THE HOUSEHOLD HANDBOOK

Answers and Solutions You Need to Know

by the
Meadowbrook Reference Group

Meadowbrook Press
18318 Minnetonka Boulevard
Deephaven, Minnesota 55391

First printing November 1981
Second printing March 1982

Printed in the United States of America

Library of Congress Cataloging in Publication Data

Main entry under title:

The Household handbook.

    Includes bibliographical references and index.
    1. Home economics—Handbooks, manuals, etc.

I.   Grady, Tom, 1951–   II. Rood, Amy,
1956–   .
TX158.H647   640   81–17226
ISBN 0–915658—46–1   AACR2
ISBN 0–915668—41–0 (pbk.)

ISBN (paperback): 0–915658–41–0
ISBN (hardcover): 0–915658–46–1

Copyright © 1981 by Meadowbrook Press

Director: Bruce Lansky
Editor: Tom Grady
Asst. Editor: Amy Rood
Research: Louise Delagran, Mary Grady
Designer: Terry Dugan
Design Assistant: Sandra Falls
Production Manager: John Ware
Illustrator: RMR Portfolio
Consulting Editor: Kathe Grooms

Acknowledgements: Special thanks to Carol Andruskiewicz, Mary Jo Asmus, Nancy Giovinco, Jeff Herpers, Sharon Herpers, Kay Hunke, Debbie Hvass, Jennifer Olson and Nancy Palesch.

Contents

You've just cut yourself, but you can't remember where you put your first aid manual. You've run out of sour cream, and you can't remember which of your cookbooks has a substitutions chart in it. You've spilled wine on your carpet—where's that stain-removal chart you cut out of a magazine? It's tornado season and you remember reading about how to protect yourself in one, but what *are* those safety rules? One of your plants droops—should you give it more water or more light? How long can that fish you caught last week stay in the freezer?

The Household Handbook answers dozens of questions, solves hundreds of problems and gives you more practical information than ten other books combined. It's a collection of the most *useful* and *authoritative* information you can get on dozens of subjects you need to know something about—from cooking, nutrition, and first aid to housekeeping, houseplants, home repairs and home security. A whole library of books is condensed into one volume!

• It's *useful* because the information is presented in the most practical, easy-to-comprehend ways possible. *The Household Handbook* is full of hundreds of charts, tables and lists. You find what you need quickly, and you understand it at a glance.

• It's *authoritative* because the information comes from organizations that know what they're talking about: the National Weather Service, the National Fire Protection Association, the Departments of Agriculture and Energy, the American Medical Association, the National Fisheries Institute, Metropolitan Life Insurance, and many others. There's no folk wisdom here—it's tried and tested advice.

Open this book to any page and you'll find yourself learning something new or remembering something you've learned before about the basics of running a house. Keep it handy—you'll be using it often.

Chapter 1

CLEANING YOUR HOUSE

🧹 Removing Stains

While the *procedures* for removing stains from fabrics and from carpets and rugs are often different, the *materials* used are often the same. Below is a list of the supplies you should have on hand to remove stains, as well as some general tips for stain removal. The two charts that follow offer specific instructions.

Supplies checklist

- ☐ Blotting materials (paper towels, facial tissues, paper napkins, bath towels, white sheets, soft cloth)
- ☐ Ammonia
- ☐ Bar soap
- ☐ Chlorine bleach
- ☐ Drycleaning fluid (Carbona, Energine, K2r)
- ☐ Lemon juice
- ☐ Liquid hand dishwashing detergent
- ☐ Rubbing alcohol
- ☐ Turpentine
- ☐ White vinegar

Stain removal tips

• **Pretesting.** Test the stain removal treatment you plan to use on an inconspicuous portion of the fabric or carpet to be sure it won't hurt the material. Call a professional drycleaner or carpet cleaner for advice if dyes bleed or the fiber changes appearance.

• **Treatment.** Treat fabric or carpet gently. Don't rub or dab heavily at the problem area. For carpets and non-washable fabrics, apply a small amount of cleaner and work gently from the edges of the soiled area to avoid spreading the spot or stain.

FABRIC CHART

Stain	How to Remove
Grease, oil, ice cream, chocolate, gravy, egg, mayonnaise	• Run cool water over stained area, rub with liquid detergent, and then soak. Rinse and wash as you normally would. • If stain persists, rub with drycleaning solution; rinse and wash. Repeat if necessary.
Chewing gum, candle wax, adhesive tape	• Rub with ice to harden. Scrape area with fingernail or dull knife. • Wipe remaining stain with a drycleaning solvent. Let dry and then wash. • If the color of the stain remains after soaking, use a bleach* in the wash.

*Always check the care label of each item to make sure chlorine bleach is safe to use. If it is not, use an all-fabric bleach.

FABRIC CHART

Stain	How to Remove
Blood	• Soak immediately in cold water. If stain has set, soak for at least 45 min. • Rub with bar soap and then wash. • If stain persists, soak in a solution of 3 tsp. ammonia to 1 qt. cold water and then wash, using chlorine bleach.*
Milk, vomit	• Soak in a solution of 1 cup salt to 1 gal. cool water; rinse and wash. • If stain persists, apply a few drops of ammonia; rinse and wash.
Wine, liquor	• Soak in cool water. Then sponge with white vinegar. Rinse well and wash.
Catsup, tomato sauce, baby formula	• Soak in warm water with liquid dishwashing detergent and a drop of ammonia. Rinse and wash, using a bleach.*
Perspiration	• Rub with liquid detergent, rinse and wash. • If stain persists, apply ammonia or white vinegar; rinse and wash.
Urine	• Soak in a solution of equal parts white vinegar and cool water. • Wash with detergent and cool water; rinse well with clear, cool water.
Water spots	• Sponge entire stained area with white vinegar; let stand a few minutes. Rinse with clear, cool water and let dry.
Grass	• Sponge with liquid detergent and rinse. • If stain persists apply rubbing alcohol; rinse and wash.

*Always check the care label of each item to make sure chlorine bleach is safe to use. If it is not, use an all-fabric bleach.

▲ Removing Stains from Fabrics

FABRIC CHART

Stain	How to Remove
Mildew	• Scrape off mildew with fingernail or dull knife. Then wash with mild suds and sponge with alcohol. Rinse and dry. • Or wash in a bleach.* • Or rub on salt and lemon juice and let dry in sun; then rinse and dry.
Yellowing	• Soak in a solution of ½ c. chlorine bleach* and 1 tbsp. white vinegar to 1 gal. warm water. Rinse thoroughly and wash. • If stain persists, repeat treatment and let dry in sun.
Rust	• Rub with lemon juice. Let dry and then wash. • *Never* use chlorine bleach, as it will permanently set the stain.
Ballpoint pen ink	• Put an absorbent pad under the stain and blot the stain with rubbing alcohol, moving the pad frequently to a clean section and blotting until you can't get out any more ink. • Then wash, using chlorine bleach.*
Lipstick, liquid make-up, mascara	• Soak in drycleaning solution and let dry. Rinse and then wash.
Paint, varnish	• Wash out paints and varnishes *before* they dry. Soak in turpentine (unless fabric is acetate). Rinse and wash, using extra detergent.

*Always check the care label of each item to make sure chlorine bleach is safe to use. If it is not, use an all-fabric bleach.

Sources: U.S. Dept. of Agriculture; New York State Cooperative Extension Service; *Dress Better for Less,* Vicki Audette (Meadowbrook Press, 1981).

CARPET CHART

Stain	How to Remove
Alcoholic beverages, black coffee or tea, fruit juices, soft drinks, syrup, washable ink	• Blot up spilled liquid; apply detergent solution (1 tsp. detergent to 1 cup cool water). Cool water without detergent may be effective in removing fresh stains. • When stain has been removed as completely as possible, rinse area with clean, cool water. Blot up excess liquid and dry rug or carpet.
Butter, cooking oil, hand cream, machine oil, some ball point inks	• Blot up or scrape off excess substance. • Apply liquid drycleaning solvent with clean cloth or absorbent cotton. Continue until stain is removed. • Dry rug or carpet and gently brush pile. • Or spray aerosol-type solvent, let dry and vacuum up white powdery residue.
Blood, chocolate, coffee or tea with cream, egg, gravy, ice cream, milk, salad dressing	• Blot up or scrape off excess substance. • Apply drycleaning solvent, followed by detergent solution (1 tsp. detergent to 1 cup cool water).
Animal urine	• Blot up the puddle as much as possible. • Apply several applications of clean, lukewarm water. • Then apply a solution of half white vinegar and half cool water. • Blot up excess liquid, rinse with clear water, and let spot dry. • If stain remains, apply vinegar solution and allow to remain on the stain for about 15 min. Blot up, rinse, and dry carpet.
Cigarette burns	• For small burns on *wool pile,* use small, sharp scissors to carefully snip away charred fibers. Then apply detergent solution; rinse and dry rug or carpet. • *Manufactured fibers* melt and cannot be repaired by this method. Usually it is necessary to cut out the burned area and replace it with a patch. In some textures, the patch will be invisible.

Note: For nail polish, rust, dye and paint stains contact a professional rug and carpet cleaner.

Source: Cooperative Extension Service of the Northeast States.

◢ 19 Uses for Vinegar

Use	Amount	What to Do
KITCHEN		
Cutting grease	A few drops of white vinegar	• When washing an item that is greasy or smelly, add white vinegar to the cleaning water to cut down on the grease and remove the odor.
Removing stains	Equal mixture of salt and white vinegar	• Salt and white vinegar will clean coffee and tea stains from china cups.
Cleaning glassware	½ cup white vinegar to 1 gal. water	• White vinegar added to rinse water will eliminate dull soap film from glassware and make it shine.
Freshening lunch boxes	Small amount of white vinegar	• Dampen a piece of fresh bread with white vinegar and put it in the lunch box overnight.
Cleaning stainless steel	Small amount of white vinegar	• Remove spots on your stainless-steel kitchen equipment by rubbing them with a cloth dampened with white vinegar.
Loosening tough stains	¼ cup white vinegar to 2 cups water	• To loosen hard-to-clean stains in glass, aluminum or porcelain pots or pans, boil white vinegar with water in pan. Wash in hot, soapy water.
Soaking pots and pans	Full-strength white vinegar	• Soak normal food-stained pots and pans in white vinegar for 30 min. • Rinse in hot, soapy water.

Use	Amount	What to Do
KITCHEN		
Eliminating cooking odors	1 tbsp. white vinegar to 1 cup water	• Boil white vinegar in water to eliminate unpleasant cooking odors.
Handling onions	Small amount of white vinegar	• Rub a little white vinegar on your fingers before and after slicing onions to remove the odor of onions quickly.
Cleaning jars	Small amount of white vinegar	• Rinse the peanut butter and mayonnaise jars you save with white vinegar to eliminate the odor of the former contents.
LAUNDRY		
Rinsing clothes	1 cup white vinegar	• Put a little white vinegar in your last rinse water to make sure your clothes get a thorough rinse.
Fluffing blankets	2 cups white vinegar	• Add white vinegar to a washer tub of water to make a good rinse for both cotton and wool blankets.
Removing deodorant stains	Small amount of white vinegar	• Get rid of stains left by deodorants and antiperspirants on washables by lightly rubbing with white vinegar. • Then launder as usual.

▲ 19 Uses for Vinegar

Use	Amount	What to Do
GENERAL		
Cleaning electric irons	Equal amounts of white or cider vinegar and salt	• Remove dark or burned stains from an electric iron by rubbing with white or cider vinegar and salt, heated first in a small aluminum pan. • Polish in the same way you do silver.
Rubbing varnished wood	1 tsp. white vinegar to 1 qt. lukewarm water	• Renew the luster of varnished surfaces by rubbing them with a soft, lintless cloth wrung out from a solution of white vinegar in lukewarm water. • When rubbing, follow the grain of the wood. • Finish the job by wiping the surface with a soft, dry cloth.
Eliminating tobacco odors	Small bowl of white vinegar	• Eliminate odors in smoke-filled rooms during and after a party by placing a small bowl of white vinegar in the room.
Removing fruit stains	Small amount of white vinegar	• Remove fruit stains from your hands by rubbing them with a little white vinegar; then wipe with a cloth.
Eliminating paint odors	Small bowl of white vinegar	• Absorb the odor of fresh paint by putting a small dish of white vinegar in the room.
Removing decals	Several applications of white vinegar	• Remove old decals by simply painting them with several coats of white vinegar. Give the vinegar time to soak in. • After several min., the decals should wash off easily.

Source: The Vinegar Institute.

- **Paste:** Mix 3 parts baking soda to 1 part water.
- **Solution:** Dissolve 4 tbsp. baking soda in 1 qt. of water.
- **Dry:** Sprinkle baking soda straight from the box.

Use	Amount	What to Do
KITCHEN		
Deodorizing refrigerator	1 box (1 lb.) every other month	• Tear off the top of the box, and place open in the back of the refrigerator or in a shelf on the door.
Deodorizing dishwasher	1 small handful daily	• Save water and energy by running dishwasher only after the evening meal. Once in the morning, before adding soiled dishes, sprinkle baking soda over the bottom of machine. It will absorb odors all day.
Freshening drains, garbage disposal	1 box (previously used in refrigerator)	• When a fresh box of baking soda goes into the refrigerator, recycle the contents of the old box down the drains to keep them sweet and fresh-smelling.
Soaking cooking utensils	Solution	• Let pots and pans soak in hot or warm solution; then wash. • Baking soda cleans glass, porcelain enamel and metal cookware without scratching.
Scouring burned or baked-on foods	Sprinkle dry as needed/ paste	• Scrub with baking soda sprinkled on a plastic scouring pad; rinse and dry. • Or let warm paste soak on burned area; keep wet, then scrub as needed.

🧹 15 Uses for Baking Soda

Use	Amount	What to Do
KITCHEN		
Shining silver flatware/ serving pieces	Paste	• Mix paste in small bowl and apply with a damp sponge or soft cloth. • Rub until clean; rinse and buff to a shiny gloss.
Sweetening and removing stains from coffee and teapot	Solution/dry	• Wash in solution to remove build-up of coffee oils and tea stains for better tasting brew. • To remove stained areas, shake baking soda on damp cloth or sponge. Rub until clean; rinse and dry.
Freshening coolers, plastic food containers	Solution	• Shake solution in bottle, or sponge out interior, and rinse with clear water to sweeten and clean.
BATHROOM		
Cleaning fiberglass shower stalls	Dry	• Sprinkle on damp sponge and gently scour to clean, deodorize and help remove mildew. Baking soda will not scratch the surface.
Cleaning bathtubs, toilets, tile, chrome	Dry/paste	• Shake on damp sponge and rub soiled areas until clean; rinse and buff dry. • For textured surfaces, apply paste and allow to set a few minutes. Sponge rinse and clean.

12

Use	Amount	What to Do
GENERAL		
Deodorizing cat litter	1 part baking soda to 3 parts litter	• Cover bottom of litter pan with 1 part baking soda; then cover baking soda with 3 parts litter to absorb odors for up to a week. Litter won't need replacing as often.
Improving septic system	1 cup per week	• Baking soda poured down a toilet or any household drain in the recommended amount makes the average tank of 300–750 gallons work better.
Putting out fire	Dry	• Toss handfuls at the base of flames in the event of grease, oil or electrical fires. • Do not use to put out flames in deep-fat fryers, since this could cause the grease to spatter and the fire to spread.
Deodorizing carpet, rug	Dry	• Test for color fastness in an inconspicuous area. • Sprinkle baking soda dry from the box; allow to set overnight, then vacuum.
Freshening laundry	⅓ cup	• Add baking soda to wash or rinse cycle. Clothes will be sweeter- and cleaner-smelling.

Source: Arm & Hammer, Division of Church & Dwight Co., Inc.

◪ Cleaning Cookware and Utensils

Type of Material	How to Clean
Stainless steel	• Wash by hand in hot, sudsy water or in dishwasher. Rinse and buff dry to remove water spots. • Rub burned-on foods with baking soda or a paste made of ammonia, water and a mild, non-chlorinated scouring powder.
Aluminum	• Hand washing is preferable; or wash in dishwasher, but turn it off before the drying cycle begins. • To remove stains and discolorations, boil a solution of 2–3 tbsp. of cream of tartar, lemon juice or vinegar added to 1 qt. of water in the utensil for 5–10 min.; then lightly scour with a soap-filled pad.
Cast iron	• Wash in hot, soapy water; rinse and dry immediately. Never use strong detergents or scouring powders. Never store with lid on. Remove rust with steel wool. • To season, coat with unsalted oil or shortening, heat in moderate oven for 2 hrs.
Porcelain on metal	• Wash with a sponge or cloth in warm, sudsy water or in the dishwasher (check manufacturer's instructions first). • Remove burned-on foods or stains by soaking the utensil or by using a non-abrasive cleansing powder and scrubber (such as a nylon net scrubber).
Copper	• Polish copper with various commercial copper cleaners. Or use a mixture of flour, salt, lemon juice and ammonia, or a mixture of flour and vinegar, to clean. After cleaning, wash in sudsy water, rinse and polish with a soft, clean cloth.
Tin	• Remove burned-on foods by boiling a solution of 1 qt. water and 2 tsp. baking soda in the utensil.

Type of Material	How to Clean
Pewter	• Rub with a paste made from denatured alcohol and whiting, a fine abrasive powder available in hardware stores. • Let the paste dry on the metal, then wash, rinse and buff dry with a soft cloth
Silver	• Prepare a paste of whiting (an abrasive powder available in hardware stores) and household ammonia or alcohol. • Apply paste with a damp cloth, wash, rinse and wipe dry. • A soft brush, like a mascara brush, is helpful for cleaning small crevices.
Glass	• Wash in warm, sudsy water or in dishwasher. • To remove burned-on foods, pre-soak in sudsy water with a little baking soda added; scrub with non-abrasive scrubber. • To remove coffee and tea stains, soak in a solution of 2 tbsp. liquid chlorine bleach per 1 cup of water, or soak overnight in solution of 2 tbsp. automatic dishwasher detergent to 1 pot of warm water.
Non-stick finish	• Let the utensil cool after each use; then wash in hot, sudsy water, rinse and dry. Avoid abrasive cleansers or pads. After washing in dishwasher, wipe lightly with cooking oil. • To remove stains, simmer a mixture of 1 tbsp. liquid bleach, 1 tbsp. vinegar and 1 cup water for 5–10 min. in the utensil; wash, rinse and dry.

Sources: Metal Cookware Mfrs. Assn.; New York State Cooperative Extension.

⛟ General Cleaning Around the House

Type of Surface	How to Clean
Appliances (mixers, blenders, toasters, and so on)	• Clean outside surfaces with lukewarm, sudsy water; rinse and wipe dry with a soft cloth to remove water spots. • To protect the finish, use a creamy appliance wax occasionally. • Avoid using abrasive scouring pads or cleansers. Instead, soften any dried-on material with a sudsy, wet cloth or paper towel. • Some small electrical appliances can be immersed. Check instructions.
Stoves (gas and electric)	• Wait until range has cooled to wipe up food spills and spatters with a clean, damp, soft cloth or paper towel. • If food is baked on, try rubbing with a nylon net scrubber, which won't scratch the surface. • Clean the burner holes on a gas range with a small wire, paper clip or pipe cleaner. Never use toothpicks, which might break off and clog the holes. • If the burner heads or grates are hard to get clean, soak them in a mixture of 1 cup vinegar and 1 gallon hot water for 30 min.
Ovens (not self-cleaning)	• Leave ½ cup ammonia in the oven overnight (make sure the oven is cold). In the morning, mix the ammonia with 1 qt. warm water, and use it to clean the inside walls of the oven and oven door. • If necessary, use a mild scouring powder or steel wool to remove difficult spots. (Don't scour finished metals, glass or baked-on enamel; you should only scour porcelain enamel and stainless steel.) • Use commercial oven cleaners with caution, since they can damage the surface outside and around the oven.
Refrigerators	• Clean the inside with a solution of 1 tbsp. baking soda to 1 qt. warm water. Rinse with clean water and wipe dry. • Clean the folds in the gasket seal around the door with mild, sudsy water.

Type of Surface	How to Clean
Refrigerators (continued)	• Vacuum the condenser coils or fins on the bottom or at the back of the refrigerator to help keep the refrigerator running more efficiently. • Defrost the freezer when the frost is about ¼″ thick; if you wait longer, the freezer won't work as well. Turn the control to "off" or "defrost," and place pans of warm water in freezer compartment. Don't chip at frost with a sharp object. Wash the compartment with a baking-soda solution; rinse and wipe dry.
Wooden chopping surfaces	• Disinfect the surface occasionally with a mild bleach solution, rinse, and rub it with a thin coat of mineral or salad oil.
Plastic counter tops	• Wipe up dirt with a warm, sudsy solution. • To remove a stain, first try rubbing it with baking soda and a soft, damp cloth or sponge. If the stain persists, wipe with a little bleach spread on a cloth.
Sinks and tubs	• Clean most dirt with warm, sudsy water. Avoid coarse scouring powders, which scratch the surfaces. • Remove mild stains with baking soda. • To clean old sinks and tubs that are badly stained, try soaking them with vinegar or lemon juice. • For tougher stains, use a diluted solution of oxalic acid (1 part acid to 10 parts water). Oxalic acid is poisonous, so wear protective gloves. To apply oxalic acid solution to the vertical surface under a faucet, mix it with cornmeal, making a thick paste. Apply carefully to the stain; rinse off completely with water. Don't let any of it get on the chrome hardware.
Toilet bowls	• If you use commercial toilet-bowl cleaners, do not mix them with bleach or chlorinated cleansers: the combination can form poisonous gases. • Toilet bowls can also be cleaned with sudsy water or a mild cleanser. Be sure to clean under the inside rim of the bowl.

⚟ General Cleaning Around the House

Type of Surface	How to Clean
Tile	• To remove soap spots or film from tile in the shower/bathtub area, wipe with a solution of water and a non-precipitating water softener, such as Calgon. • Try wiping the tiles with a vinegar solution (1 part vinegar to 4 parts water). Rinse with clear water and buff dry with a soft towel or cloth. • Clean the grout around the tile with a small, stiff brush; a toothbrush or a nail brush works well. If the grout is badly stained, scrub with a solution of chlorine bleach (¾ cup per 1 gallon of water).
Windows and mirrors	• Use a commercial cleaner or one of the following homemade solutions: either 1 qt. warm water and 1 tbsp. household ammonia, or 2 tbsp. vinegar and 1 qt. warm water. • Don't use soap since it may leave streaks, and don't wash windows in direct sunlight.
Walls and woodwork	• Dust surfaces first, to remove loose soil. • Wash or spot-clean *painted surfaces* with a solution of soap or mild detergent and water, or with a mild commercial household cleaner. If you use soap, soften the sudsy water and rinse water with 1 tbsp. borax per 1 qt. of water. • Do not use scouring powders, since they may remove the paint. • Wash walls from the bottom up (cleaning solution that runs down a dirty wall may cause streaks that are difficult to remove). Clean only a small area at a time; rinse with clear water and then go on to another spot overlapping the area. Dry with a soft cloth or towel. • Test the washability of a *wallcovering* in an inconspicuous place. If washable, use a mild detergent and cool water, and follow instructions above. • If wallcoverings are nonwashable, they can be cleaned by rubbing gently with art gum (a dough-type wallpaper cleaner), available in hardware stores.

Type of Surface	How to Clean
Lampshades	• Dust with a clean, soft cloth or the dusting attachment of your vacuum cleaner. • *Fiberglass, plastic and other washable shades:* wipe with a clean, damp cloth. • *Silk, rayon, nylon and other washable shades that have been sewn to the frame and have colorfast trimmings:* dip them in a tub of mild, lukewarm suds; rinse in clean, lukewarm water. Dry quickly to prevent frames from rusting and staining fabric. Do not dry silk shades in direct sun; drying in front of a fan speeds up the process. • *Linen, cotton and hand-painted shades or shades with glued-on trim:* don't wash them in water. Use a dough-type wallpaper cleaner, available in hardware stores.
Venetian blinds	• Dust blinds regularly with dusting mitts or clean, absorbent gloves, or use a Venetian blind brush, which cleans several blinds at once. • Or tilt blinds flat and go over them with the dusting attachment of a vacuum cleaner. • Dip painted or plastic blinds in a tub of warm suds, or wash them individually after they've been removed from the tapes.
Window shades	• Clean washable shades by spreading them unrolled on a clean, flat surface and scrubbing with a brush or cloth wrung out in warm, sudsy water. Try not to wet the shade very much. Dry thoroughly before rerolling. • Clean nonwashable shades with art gum, cornmeal or a dough-type wallpaper cleaner.

Sources: U.S. Dept. of Agriculture, New York State Cooperative Extension Service.

⚜ Cleaning Furniture

Type of Furniture	How to Clean
Bamboo, cane, wicker, reed	• Wash with a cloth or brush and sudsy water. If the furniture's very soiled, add a little ammonia to the sudsy water. Rinse with clean water and dry thoroughly.
Upholstered fabric	• Dust with your vacuum cleaner, a whisk broom or a coarse cloth. (If the cushions are down-filled—and aren't lined with down-proof ticking—they should be brushed, not vacuumed.) • Shampoo using detergent foam or suds to avoid wetting the furniture padding. Always test for shrinkage, fading or color bleeding on the back or in an inconspicuous area. Work quickly, a small area at a time. • To speed up drying, set furniture outdoors in the shade, indoors with windows open, or in front of an electric fan or heater. • To remove stains from fabrics, see procedures on pp. 4 – 6.
Upholstered leather	• Rub briskly with a lather made from warm water and castile or saddle soap. Wipe with a clean, damp cloth. Rub with a soft, dry cloth to restore sheen. • Do not use oils, furniture polishes or varnishes on leather—they may contain solvents that can make leather sticky.
Upholstered vinyl	• Sponge with warm water and a mild detergent solution. Allow the solution to soak a few minutes. Rub to loosen soil. Rinse with clear water and dry with a clean cloth or towel. • Do not use scouring powder, steel wool or strong household cleaners. • Use vinyl cleaners to remove grease and oily spots. • To remove other stains, try sponging the area with equal parts denatured alcohol and water, or with rubbing alcohol as it comes from the bottle; then apply saddle soap. Rinse with clear water and blot with a towel or soft cloth.

Type of Furniture	How to Clean

Wood

Regular care

- Dust with a dry, lint-free cloth or the dust attachment of the vacuum cleaner. Add a few drops of furniture polish to the cloth, if you'd like, to help pick up dust. Move the cloth or the vacuum cleaner in the direction of the wood grain.
- Water and liquids should never be allowed to stand on wooden surfaces; blot spills up quickly with a clean, dry cloth.

Waxing and polishing

- Because finishes vary, your best guide is to follow the manufacturer's directions. If they are not available, the advice below may be helpful, but be sure to test the products you use on an inconspicuous spot before proceeding.
- *High luster or shine:* select a liquid polish or paste wax that indicates it will dry to a high shine.
- *Low luster or satin finish:* select a greaseless cream polish or wax that protects the finish without increasing the shine.
- *Natural oil finish:* re-oil occasionally with the type of oil used by the manufacturer, or rub with boiled linseed oil.
- Once you have selected a product, do not switch back and forth.
- Don't use waxes and polishes too frequently, as they may produce a film; this film can be removed by wiping the surface with a cloth dampened with mineral spirits or synthetic turpentine.

Removing spots, rings and candle wax

- To remove white spots or rings, sprinkle cigarette ashes, salt or rottenstone (available in hardware stores) over the spot. Rub gently in the direction of the wood grain with a cloth dipped in mineral or linseed oil. Wipe dry with a clean cloth. Repolish, wax or oil with the product you have been using.
- To remove candle wax, scrape off as much as you can with your fingers, a soft kitchen scraper or a stick. Wipe any remaining spot with a cloth dipped in mineral oil or drycleaning fluid. Repolish, wax or oil.

Source: New York State Cooperative Extension Service.

▲ Caring for Your Floors

WASHING

Type of Surface	How to Clean
Linoleum, rubber, vinyl, stone, concrete, ceramic asphalt, marble	• Clean occasionally with a mop or cloth wrung out in water. A little mild detergent or household cleaner may be used. • Do not use harsh abrasives or strong alkaline cleaners. • Avoid wetting the floor too much, especially a floor with lots of seams.
Wood, cork	• Clean with a solvent such as turpentine, nontoxic drycleaning fluid, or a liquid- or paste-solvent cleaning wax. • Do not use water, unless otherwise directed by manufacturer of floor finish.

WAXING/FINISHING

Type of Surface	How to Wax/Finish
Linoleum, rubber, vinyl	• Use water-base waxes and finishes on any surface not damaged by water. Most are self-polishing. • To remove any wax build-up, follow the directions on the container or wipe with a solution of household ammonia and water (1 cup ammonia per 1 gallon of water).
Wood, cork	• Use spirit-solvent waxes, which are available in paste and liquid forms. Most need to be polished or buffed.

Source: New York State Cooperative Extension Service.

Washing and Drying Fabrics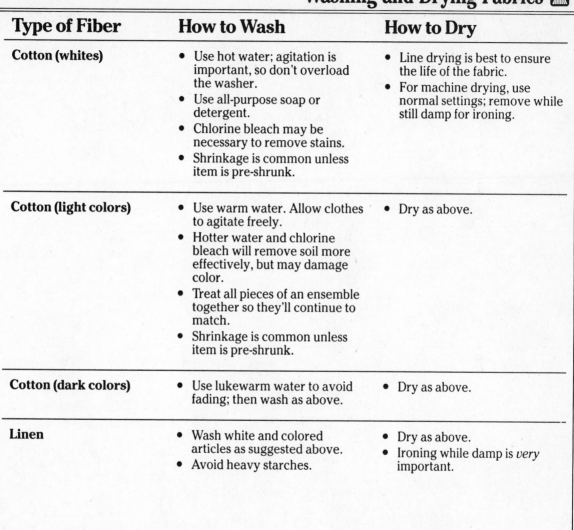

Type of Fiber	How to Wash	How to Dry
Cotton (whites)	• Use hot water; agitation is important, so don't overload the washer. • Use all-purpose soap or detergent. • Chlorine bleach may be necessary to remove stains. • Shrinkage is common unless item is pre-shrunk.	• Line drying is best to ensure the life of the fabric. • For machine drying, use normal settings; remove while still damp for ironing.
Cotton (light colors)	• Use warm water. Allow clothes to agitate freely. • Hotter water and chlorine bleach will remove soil more effectively, but may damage color. • Treat all pieces of an ensemble together so they'll continue to match. • Shrinkage is common unless item is pre-shrunk.	• Dry as above.
Cotton (dark colors)	• Use lukewarm water to avoid fading; then wash as above.	• Dry as above.
Linen	• Wash white and colored articles as suggested above. • Avoid heavy starches.	• Dry as above. • Ironing while damp is *very* important.

⬛ Washing and Drying Fabrics

Type of Fiber	How to Wash	How to Dry
Silk	• Dryclean or hand wash in warm water with a mild detergent promptly after wearing to prevent perspiration damage. • Choose an oxygen bleach if needed.	• Never use the dryer, which will cause yellowing. • Dry by rolling the article in an absorbent towel and then squeezing out the excess moisture. • Finish drying in normal room temperature air.
Wool	• Wash by hand or by machine with a mild detergent in cool water with some agitation (use a gentle cycle) or in warm water without agitation. • Dryclean to avoid shrinkage or *pilling* (formation of little balls of fiber on the surface of the article).	• Most woolens should not be dryer dried. • Roll the article in an absorbent towel, squeeze (*don't* wring) out excess moisture, and then pull the article into shape. • Allow it to finish drying on a flat surface in room temperature air. • Handle carefully when wet.
Nylon, acrylic, polyester	• Rub detergent on soiled spots before washing in warm water. Use gentle agitation. • Turn garments inside out to minimize pilling. • Put delicate items in a net bag when machine washing. • Wash white garments with other whites only. • Use chlorine bleach if fabrics are stained.	• Use the permanent press cycle, if your dryer has one. • Keep the load small so that items will tumble freely. • Keep them inside out to avoid pilling. • Remove clothes immediately after tumbling stops. Fold or hang right away.

Washing and Drying Fabrics ▲

Type of Fiber	How to Wash	How to Dry
Acetate, triacetate	• Drycleaning is recommended unless label indicates fabric is washable. • Pre-treat soiled places with detergent or soap. • Wash with a light-duty product. • Handle gently to avoid stretching; don't twist or wring garments.	• Dry at low temperature in machine or in normal room temperature air.
Rayon	• Hand wash delicate rayons in warm water. • Squeeze gently; do not twist or wring. • Heavier rayons can be washed in hot water with heavy-duty detergent.	• Drying for too long a time at too high a temperature may result in shrinkage and static electricity. • Remove from dryer while slightly damp and pull into shape.
Spandex	• Use warm water and detergent. • Avoid chlorine bleach.	• Dry at low temperature.
Rubber	• Wash often at low temperature to remove oily soils. • Avoid bleach.	• Dry at moderate temperature.
Blends	• A blend will take on the qualities of the fibers used in its production. Know what those combinations are. The best cleaning and drying guides are the labels or leaflets on care that most manufacturers attach to their merchandise.	

Sources: U.S. Dept. of Commerce, National Bureau of Standards; New York State Cooperative Extension Service; Association of Home Appliance Mfrs.

COOKING

How to Save Money at the Supermarket

1. **Shop with a purpose and with a list.** Plan your menus for the entire week (or 2), and then organize your shopping list so that you have to pass through each section of the supermarket only once. If you have to return to the first aisle to pick up just one thing, you may find yourself attracted by other items.

2. **Try to control your impulse buying.** One study has estimated that almost 50% of purchases are entirely unplanned. Be especially careful at the start of your shopping trip, when your cart is nearly empty. You're more susceptible to high-priced, unplanned purchases then.

3. **Get your shopping done within a half hour.** Supermarkets are often very comfortable places to linger in, but one study suggests that customers spend at least 50 cents a minute after a half hour in the store.

4. **Shop alone if you can.** How many unplanned purchases are made when you've got "help"?

5. **Never shop when you're hungry.**

6. **Use coupons wisely.** Food companies often use coupon offers to promote either new products or old products that haven't been selling well. Ask yourself if you would have bought the item had there been no coupon, and compare prices with competing brands to see if you're really saving money.

7. **Be a smart shopper.** Be aware that grocery stores stock the highest-priced items at eye level. The lower-priced staples like flour, sugar and salt are often below eye level, as are bulk quantities of many items. Also be aware that foods displayed at the end of an aisle may appear to be on sale, but often are not.

8. **Use unit pricing** to find the brand and container-size of food that costs the least per pound, ounce or pint.

9. **Avoid foods that are packaged as individual servings.** Extra packaging usually boosts the price of the product.

10. **When buying meat, consider the amount of lean meat in the cut, as well as the price per pound.** A relatively high-priced cut with little or no waste may provide more meat for your money than a low-priced cut with a great deal of bone, gristle or fat. Chicken and turkey are often bargains compared to other meats, and fish is usually a good buy too.

11. **Buy vegetables and fruits in season** since they'll be at their peak of quality and their lowest price. Never buy the first crop; prices are sure to go down.

Sources: U.S. Dept. of Agriculture; Univ. of Vermont Extension Service; *Nutrition Action* (published by the Center for Science in the Public Interest; membership is available to the public for $20.00 per year).

Vegetable Buying and Storing Guide ⬚

Vegetable	What to Look for	Peak Season	Storage
Artichokes	Plump globes that are heavy in relation to size, with thick, tightly clinging, olive-green scales. *Avoid:* those with areas of brown on the scales.	April-May	Store in a plastic bag in the refrigerator; eat within 3–5 days.
Asparagus	Closed, compact tips with smooth, round spears. A rich green should cover most of the spear.	March-May	Store in the refrigerator (do not wash first); eat within 2–3 days.
Beans, Snap	Firm, crisp, slender pods with good green color.	April-Sept.	Store in the refrigerator; use within 1 week.
Beets	Firm, round, smooth beets with a deep red color. Wilted or decayed tops indicate a lack of freshness, but the roots may be satisfactory if firm.	All year	Remove the tops; store in the refrigerator; use within 2 weeks.
Broccoli	A firm, compact cluster of small flower buds. Color ranges from dark and sage green to purplish-green, depending on variety. *Avoid:* wilted or yellow leaves, thick stems and soft spots on the bud cluster.	All year	Store in the refrigerator; use within 3–5 days.
Brussels Sprouts	A fresh, bright-green color, tight-fitting outer leaves and firm body. *Avoid:* small holes or ragged leaves, which may indicate worm injury.	Oct.-Jan.	Store in the refrigerator; use within 3–5 days.
Cabbages (green cabbage, Savoy cabbage and red cabbage)	Firm or hard heads that are heavy for their size. Outer leaves should be a good green or red color (depending on type) and free from serious blemishes.	All year	Store in the refrigerator; use within 1–2 weeks.
Carrots	Firm, well-shaped roots with good orange color. *Avoid:* large green areas at top.	All year	Store in the refrigerator; use within 2 weeks.

🗂 Vegetable Buying and Storing Guide

Vegetable	What to Look for	Peak Season	Storage
Cauliflower	White to creamy-white, compact, solid and clean curds (the white, edible portion). Size bears no relation to quality. Ignore small green leaflets extending through curd. *Avoid:* smudgy or speckled curd or many discolored spots.	Sept.-Jan.	Store in the refrigerator; use within 2 weeks.
Celery	Crisp, light- or medium-green stalks that are thick and solid with a glossy surface.	All year	Store in the refrigerator; use within 1 week.
Corn	Green husks, and ears that are covered with small, medium-yellow kernels. Stem ends (opposite from the silk) should not be too discolored or dried. Select corn that is cold to the touch.	May-Sept.	Store, unhusked and uncovered, in the refrigerator; use as soon as possible for sweetest flavor.
Cucumbers	Firm cucumbers of medium size with good green color. Good cucumbers typically have many small lumps on their surfaces and may also have some white or greenish-white color. *Avoid:* withered or shriveled ends.	All year	Wash, dry and store in the refrigerator; use within 1 week.
Eggplants	Firm, heavy, smooth eggplants with uniformly dark purple to purple-black skin. *Avoid:* those with irregular dark brown spots.	All year	Store at cool room temperature (around 60° F.). Temperature below 50° F. may cause chilling injury.
Endive, Escarole and Chicory	Cold, crisp, green leavs. *Avoid:* reddish discoloration of the hearts.	All year	Wash, drain and store in the refrigerator; use within 1 week.
Garlic	Firm, plump bulbs with clean, dry, unbroken skins.	All year	Store open in a cool, dry place; do not refrigerate; use within 1 month.

Vegetable Buying and Storing Guide 🗂

Vegetable	What to Look for	Peak Season	Storage
Greens (spinach, kale, collards, chard)	Crisp, green leaves. *Avoid:* coarse stems or soft, yellowing leaves.	All year	Wash in cold water, drain well, store in plastic bags or crisper in refrigerator; use within 3–5 days.
Lettuce *Iceberg*	Large, round and solid heads that "give" slightly when squeezed. Outer leaves should be medium-green; inner leaves are lighter in color.	All year	Remove core and rinse end up under cold, running water. Drain thoroughly. Store in a tightly closed plastic bag.
Boston and bibb	Smaller head with light-green leaves.	All year	Wash and drain well. Store in crisper or plastic bag in fridge. Use within 3–5 days.
Romaine	Crisp, dark-green leaves in loosely folded head.	All year	As above.
Leaf	Broad, loose and fairly smooth leaves that vary in color with variety.	All year	As above.
Mushrooms	Small to medium mushrooms with white, cream-colored or tan caps. Caps should either be closed around the stem or moderately open with pink or light-tan gills.	All year	Store in the crisper in a paper bag or covered with a damp paper towel. Use within 5 days.
Okra	Tender, bright-green pods (the tips will bend with very slight pressure) 2–4½″ long.	May-Sept.	Store in a plastic bag in the refrigerator; use within 3–5 days.
Onions (dry)	Hard or firm globes with dry, crackly skins and small necks. *Avoid:* green spots: wet, soggy necks; sprouts.	All year	Store at room temperature, or slightly cooler, in loosely woven or open-mesh containers; will keep for several months.

◻ Vegetable Buying and Storing Guide

Vegetable	What to Look for	Peak Season	Storage
Onions (green) *Scallions Leeks*	Bunches with crisp, green tops and white portions extending 2–3″ up from the bulb end.	All year	Store in a plastic bag in the refrigerator; use within 3–5 days.
Parsley	Crisp, bright-green leaves.	All year	Store in a plastic bag in the refrigerator; use within 3–5 days.
Parsnips, Turnips	Smooth, firm, well-shaped roots of small to medium width.	May-Sept.	Remove tops; store in plastic bags in the refrigerator; use within 2 weeks.
Peppers (sweet bell, red, chili)	Firm peppers with relatively heavy weight, glossy sheen and bright-green color (which may be tinged with red). *Avoid:* soft, watery spots on sides and thin walls.	All year	Wash, dry and store in the crisper or in plastic bags in the refrigerator; use within 1 week.
Potatoes *New* (best used for boiling or creaming) *General purpose* (used for boiling, frying and baking) *Baking*	Firm, well-shaped, reasonably smooth potatoes. *Avoid:* green discoloration and sprouts.	All year	Never refrigerate; store in a dark, dry place with good ventilation, with a temperature of about 45–50° F. Will keep, in this manner, for months.
Radishes	Plump, round, firm, medium-size (¾–1⅛″ in diameter) radishes with good red color. *Avoid:* very large radishes or those with yellow tops.	All year	Remove tops; store in a plastic bag in the refrigerator; use within 2 weeks.

Vegetable Buying and Storing Guide 🗂

Vegetable	What to Look for	Peak Season	Storage
Rutabagas	Firm, smooth, round or moderately elongated rutabagas with relatively heavy weight for their size. Size is not important. *Avoid:* deep cuts or punctures.	May-Oct.	Store at cool room temperature (around 60° F.); will keep for several months.
Squash (summer) *Crookneck* *Straightneck* *Patty pan* *Zucchini*	Small to medium, well-developed, firm squash with a glossy skin. *Avoid:* dull, tough surface.	May-Sept.	Store in crisper or plastic bags in the refrigerator; use within 5–8 days.
Squash (winter) *Acorn* *Butternut* *Hubbard* *Delicious* *Banana* *Buttercup*	Hard, tough rind; heavy weight for its size. Slight variations in skin color are not important. *Avoid:* soft areas, sunburnt spots, or cuts.	Sept.-Feb.	Don't refrigerate; store at cool room temperature (around 60° F.); will keep for several months.
Sweet Potatoes	Thick, medium-sized, firm sweet potatoes with smooth, bright, uniformly colored skins. *Avoid:* any cuts or blemishes.	Sept.-April	Don't refrigerate; store at cool room temperature (around 60° F.); will keep for several months. Handle gently to avoid bruising.
Tomatoes	Smooth, firm and plump tomatoes with an overall rich, red color. *Avoid:* green or yellow areas or cracks near the stem scar as well as soft, water-soaked spots or depressed areas.	All year	Store ripe tomatoes in a cool, dark place and use as soon as possible. Keep unripe tomatoes at room temperature away from direct sunlight until they ripen. Putting them in a brown paper bag hastens ripening.

Sources: U.S. Dept. of Agriculture; Lunds, Inc., Minneapolis.

▢ Fruit Buying and Storing Guide

Fruit	What to Look for	Peak Season	Ripening/ Storage
Apples	Firm, crisp fruit with good color for the variety. *Avoid:* discoloration, shriveling, apples that yield to slight pressure on the skin.	All year, depending on the variety (see pp. 39–40)	Keep in refrigerator or cool, dark place. Use ripe fruit within 1 week.
Apricots	Plump, well-formed, fairly firm fruit with deep-yellow or yellowish-orange color.	June-July	Store in paper bag in a warm room to ripen. Then keep in refrigerator for 3–5 days.
Avocado	Color ranging from purple-black to green, depending on variety. Irregular brown marks on the surface do not affect quality. *Avoid:* dark, sunken spots or cracked surfaces.	All year	Hold at room temperature for a few days to ripen. Ripe when flesh is slightly soft and yields to gentle pressure. Refrigerate ripe fruit and use as soon as possible.
Bananas	Firm, plump fruit. Color ranges from green to brown: best-eating quality is reached when the skin is solid yellow specked with brown. *Avoid:* grayish-yellow or bruised fruit.	All year	Ripen at 70° F. room temperature; when at stage of preferred ripeness, refrigerate and use as soon as possible.
Blueberries	Plump, firm, dry berries. Color should be dark blue with a silvery bloom. *Avoid:* baskets showing signs of bruised or leaking fruit.	May-Sept.	Pack loosely, cover and refrigerate immediately. Use as soon as possible.
Cantaloupe	Yellowish cast to the rind, with veining that is thick and coarse. Fruit should have no stem and should give slightly at the blossom end when pressed gently. Ripe cantaloupes have a pleasant odor. *Avoid:* a pronounced yellow rind color, large bruises and a softening over the entire rind.	May-Sept.	Hold at room temperature for a few days to ripen; then refrigerate and use as soon as possible.

Vegetable	What to Look for	Peak Season	Storage
Casaba Melon	Golden-yellow rind with a slight softening at the blossom end. They have no odor. *Avoid:* dark, water-soaked spots.	July-Nov.	Hold at room temperature for a few days to ripen; then refrigerate and use as soon as possible.
Cherries	Plump, glossy fruit with dark color ranging from deep red to black. Firm but not hard. *Avoid:* dried stems, shrivelling, and leaking flesh.	May-Aug.	Will ripen at room temperature. Refrigerate ripe fruit immediately and use within 2 days.
Cranberries	Plump, firm, red to reddish-black berries.	Sept.-Jan.	Refrigerate and use within 1½ weeks. For longer storage, freeze in original package.
Crenshaw Melon	Deep golden-yellow rind that yields slightly to thumb pressure. Pleasant odor when ripe. *Avoid:* sunken, water-soaked spots.	Aug.-Sept.	Hold at room temperature for a few days to ripen; then refrigerate and use as soon as possible.
Grapefruit	Firm, thick-skinned, globular fruit that is heavy for its size. Skin defects—green tinge, scars, etc.—do not affect quality. *Avoid:* soft, discolored areas on peel at stem end; loose or wrinkled skin.	Jan.-May	Refrigerate or leave at room temperature. Use within 2 weeks.
Grapes	Plump, firm grapes that are securely attached to green, pliable stems. Green grapes are sweetest when yellowish-green in color. *Avoid:* wrinkled or leaking berries, grapes with bleached areas around stem.	July-Nov.	Grapes are usually ripe when shipped to market but will ripen further at room temperature. Refrigerate ripe fruit immediately and use as soon as possible.

⬚ Fruit Buying and Storing Guide

Fruit	What to Look for	Peak Season	Ripening/ Storage
Honeydew Melon	Creamy or yellowish-white rind with a velvety or waxy feel, distinctive melon aroma. *Avoid:* dead-white or greenish-white color and hard, smooth rind.	June-Oct.	Hold at room temperature to ripen; then refrigerate and use as soon as possible.
Lemons	Fruit that is heavy for its size with fairly smooth-textured skin. *Avoid:* shrivelled skin, soft spots.	All year	Keep at room temperature or refrigerate. Use within 2 weeks.
Limes	Fruit heavy for its size with bright-green, glossy skin. *Avoid:* dull, dry skin.	All year	Keep at room temperature or refrigerate. Use within 2 weeks.
Mangos	Green skin with yellowish to red areas (these increase with ripeness). *Avoid:* grayish skin discoloration, pitting or black spots.	May-Aug.	Keep at room temperature until very soft. Then refrigerate and use as soon as possible.
Nectarines	Orange-yellow color between red areas, slight softening of the fruit around the stem end. *Avoid:* hard, dull or shrivelled fruit.	June-Sept.	Hold at room temperature to ripen; then refrigerate and use within 3–5 days.
Oranges	Firm and heavy oranges with finely textured skin. Green skin color or russeting (brown or black mottling or speckling over skin) does not affect quality. *Avoid:* very rough or dull, dry skin; soft spots.	All year	Store at room temperature or refrigerate. Use within 2 weeks.
Papayas	Medium, well-sized fruit that is at least half yellow.	May-June; Oct.-Dec.	Ripen at room temperature until skin is primarily golden; then refrigerate and use as soon as possible.

Fruit	What to Look for	Peak Season	Ripening/ Storage
Peaches	Fairly firm or slightly soft fruit with a yellowish or cream-colored background skin color (between red patches). *Avoid:* green, hard peaches or those with large bruises.	June-Sept.	Hold at room temperature to soften; then refrigerate promptly and use within 3–5 days.
Pears	Fairly firm fruit. *Bartletts:* pale to rich yellow color; *Anjou/Comice:* light to yellowish green; *Bosc:* greenish to brownish yellow. Russeting (brown speckling) does not affect quality. *Avoid:* shriveled fruit with dull skin and slight weakening of the flesh near the stem.	*Bartlett:* Aug.-Nov.; *Anjou, Bosc, Comice:* Nov.-May	Hold at room temperature in a closed paper bag until stem end yields to pressure; then refrigerate and use within 3–5 days.
Persian Melon	Yellowish cast to the rind and veining that is thick and coarse. Fruit should have no stem and should give slightly at the blossom end when pressed gently.	Aug.-Sept.	Hold at room temperature until ripe; then refrigerate and use as soon as possible.
Persimmons	Plump, smooth, highly colored fruit with a green cap.	Oct.-Dec.	Keep at room temperature until soft; then refrigerate and use as soon as possible.
Pineapples	Plump, glossy eyes or pips; firmness; a lively color (golden-yellow, orange-yellow or reddish-brown depending on the variety); leaves or spikes that pull out easily; fruit that is heavy for its size; a rich, sweet smell. *Avoid:* watery or dark eyes; dull, yellowish-green color.	April-May	Ripen at room temperature (normally within 3 days). Then refrigerate and use as soon as possible. Ripen and store crown-side down.
Plums	Good color for the variety with fairly firm to slightly soft flesh. *Avoid:* skin breaks; brownish discoloration; hard, shriveled or leaking fruit.	June-Sept.	Hold at room temperature until flesh yields to pressure; then refrigerate and use within 3–5 days.

▣ Fruit Buying and Storing Guide

Fruit	What to Look for	Peak Season	Ripening/ Storage
Pomegranates	Pink or bright red rind. *Avoid:* dry-looking fruits.	Sept.-Nov.	Keep cold and humid.
Prunes	(Same as plums)	Aug.-Oct.	(Same as plums)
Raspberries (blackberries, dewberries, loganberries, youngberries)	Bright, clean berries with uniform good color. *Avoid:* those with attached stem caps, leaky or moldy berries (look for stained spots on containers).	June-Aug.	Refrigerate immediately and use as soon as possible.
Rhubarb	Firm, bright stems with large amounts of pink or red color. *Avoid:* very slender or very thick stems, wilted stalks.	Jan.-July	Store in refrigerator; use within 3–5 days.
Strawberries	Firm, dry, full-red berries with bright luster and green caps still attached. *Avoid:* berries with large seedy areas, a shrunken appearance or mold.	April-June	Refrigerate immediately, unwashed, with caps intact; hull and wash just before using.
Tangerines	Deep yellow or orange color, fruit that is heavy for its size. A puffy appearance and feel are normal. *Avoid:* cut skin or soft spots.	Dec.-Jan.	Refrigerate and use as soon as possible.
Watermelon	*Whole:* firm, smooth melons with a dullness on the rind. Underside should be yellowish or cream-white; ends of melon should be filled out. *Avoid:* stark-white or greenish-colored undersides. *Cut:* firm, red, juicy flesh with black seeds. *Avoid:* white streaks in flesh, whiteish seeds.	June-Aug.	Keep at room temperature or refrigerate; use within 3–5 days.

Sources: U.S. Dept. of Agriculture; Lunds, Inc., Minneapolis.

Variety	When in Season	What They're Like	Raw	General Cooking	Baking Whole
Beacon	Aug.-Sept.	Medium; red; mild.		•	•
Cortland	Sept.-Feb.	Medium to large; bright red with stripes; juicy, slightly tart, tender, crisp, fragrant.	•	•	•
Golden Delicious	Sept.-June	Medium to large; yellow; sweet, semi-firm, crisp.	•	•	•
Granny Smith	Nov.-June	Medium to large; bright green; moderately tart, juicy, crisp.	•	•	•
Gravenstein	Aug.-Oct.	Medium; yellow; firm, tart, juicy, spicy.	•	•	
Greening	Oct.-April	Large; green or yellow; firm, crisp.		•	•
Haralson	Oct.-March	Medium, red; tart, juicy.	•	•	•
Jonathan	Sept.-April	Small to medium; deep red; juicy, moderately tart, tender, crisp, fragrant.	•	•	•
McIntosh	Sept.-April	Medium to large; bright dark red with stripes; juicy, slightly tart, tender, crisp, fragrant.	•	•	•
Newtown Pippin	Sept.-May	Small to medium; yellow-green; firm, mildly tart.	•	•	•
Prairie Spy	Oct.-April	Medium to large; bright red with stripes; very juicy, moderately tart, tender, crisp, fragrant.	•	•	•
Red Delicious	Sept.-June	Medium to large; deep red; 5 knobs on blossom end; sweet, tender, fragrant.	•		
Rome Beauty	Oct.-July	Large; yellow mingled with red; juicy, slightly tart, firm, crisp.	•	•	•
Spartan	Oct.-May	Medium; deep red; firm, crisp, juicy.	•	•	

☐ Apple Buying Guide

Variety	When in Season	What They're Like	Where to Use		
			Raw	General Cooking	Baking Whole
Staymen	Oct.-June	Medium to large; dull red with stripes; juicy, tart. semifirm, crisp.	●	●	●
Wealthy	Sept.-Nov.	Medium; striped red; crisp, juicy.	●	●	
Winesap	Oct.-Sept.	Small to medium; deep bright red with small scattered white dots; very juicy, slightly tart, firm, crisp, fragrant.	●	●	●
Yellow Newton	Sept.-June	Medium; yellow; juicy, moderately tart.	●	●	
York Imperial	Oct.-June	Medium to large; light or purplish red over yellow; usually lopsided in shape; slightly tart, firm, crisp.		●	●

Sources: U.S. Dept. of Agriculture.

All About Beans, Peas and Lentils 🗂

| **Storing** | • After packages are opened, dry beans, peas and lentils should be stored in tightly covered containers and kept in a cool, dry place. |
| | • Cooked beans should be tightly covered and stored in the refrigerator; use within a day or two. |

Soaking	• Dry beans and whole peas should be soaked before cooking; lentils and split peas used in soups may be cooked without soaking.
	• Always wash beans thoroughly before soaking.
	• *Traditional method.* To 1 lb. (1½–2 cups) of dry beans or peas, add 6 cups cold water and 1½ tsp. salt. Let stand overnight or for 6–8 hrs. Drain and rinse before cooking.
	• *Quick method.* To 1 lb. (1½–2 cups) of dry beans or peas, add 6–8 cups hot water with or without 1½ tsp. salt. Heat; let boil 3 min.; cover and set aside for 1 hr. Drain, rinse and cool before cooking.
	• Be sure that whatever pot you use to soak the beans or peas in is large enough to allow them to expand 2½ times.

| **Cooking** | • *Standard method.* Put soaked beans, peas or lentils into a good-sized kettle. If you start with 1 lb. (1½–2 cups) of dried beans, add 6 cups hot water (or to about 1 in. above the beans). Add 2 tsp. oil or butter and 2 tsp. salt. Simmer gently until they are done (generally 1½–2 hrs.). |
| | • *Savory method.* Follow directions above, but use 2 tsp. onion salt and ¼ tsp. garlic salt instead of plain salt. Add 1 tbsp. chicken stock, or 3–4 bouillon cubes, and ¼ tsp. white pepper. |

| **Yield** | • 1 lb. = 1½ cups, dry = 5–6 cups, cooked. |

Sources: U.S. Dept. of Agriculture, California Dry Bean Advisory Board.

🗒 All About Rice and Pasta

RICE

Cooking

- *Top-of-the-range method.* In a 2- or 3-quart saucepan, combine 1 cup uncooked rice with 2 cups liquid (2½ cups for brown rice), 1 tbsp. butter and 1 tsp. salt. Bring the ingredients to a boil and stir once or twice. Lower heat to simmer and cover pan tightly. Cook for 15 min. (45 min. for brown rice) or until rice is tender and liquid is absorbed.
- *Oven method.* In a baking dish, combine 1 cup uncooked rice with 2 cups boiling liquid (2½ cups for brown rice), 1 tbsp. butter and 1 tsp. salt. Cover dish tightly and bake at 350°F. for 25–30 min. (1 hr. for brown rice).

Tips

- For drier rice, use 2 tbsp. less liquid; or, after cooking, fluff rice with fork and let stand, covered, for 5–10 min.
- When reheating rice, add 2 tbsp. liquid for each cup. Cover; heat for 5 min.

Yield

- 1 cup uncooked, white or brown = 3–4 cups, cooked.

Source: Rice Council of America.

PASTA

Cooking

- To 3 qts. rapidly boiling water, gradually add 8 oz. pasta along with 2 tsp. salt. Make sure water continues to boil as you add pasta. Cook, uncovered, stirring occasionally. Don't overcook. Cook "al dente" (tender to the tooth)—5–10 min. is generally enough. Drain in colander. Rinse only when making salads.

Tips

- To keep pasta from sticking together, add 1 tbsp. olive oil to cooking water.
- 1 lb. of pasta requires 4–6 qts. of water for cooking.

Yield

- 1 lb. uncooked spaghetti = 6½ cups, cooked.

Source: National Pasta Assn.

Storing

- Nuts will keep in the shell at room temperature for short periods of time; for prolonged storage, keep them in a cool, dry place.
- Shelled nuts will keep fresh for several months when refrigerated in tightly closed containers.
- Shelled or unshelled nuts will keep for up to a year when frozen in tightly closed containers.

Removing skins

- *Blanching* is the best method for almonds, peanuts and chestnuts. Place nuts in boiling water and let stand 2–3 min. Drain. Slide skin off with your fingers. Spread nuts on absorbent paper to dry.
- *Roasting* is the best method for filberts. Spread nuts in single layer in shallow baking pan. Bake at 300° F. for 10–15 min. or until heated through; stir occasionally. Cool slightly, and slip skins off with your fingers.

Roasting or toasting

- To roast, spread nuts on baking sheet and heat in oven for 5–15 min. at 350° F. or until lightly browned; stir occasionally.
- To toast, heat nutmeats slowly on top of range for 10–15 min. or until lightly browned; stir occasionally.
- Nuts continue to brown slightly after being removed from heat, so avoid overbrowning.

Yields

- 1 lb. unshelled nuts will yield the following amounts (by weight and volume) of shelled nuts:

	Oz.	Cups
Almonds, whole	6⅓	1¼
Brazil nuts, whole	7⅔	1½
Filberts, whole	7⅓	1½
Peanuts, roasted	11⅔	2¼
Pecans, halved	8½	2¼
Walnuts, chopped	3½	¾
Walnuts, halved	7¼	2

Source: U.S. Dept. of Agriculture.

🗂 Safe Food Storage Guide

Food	Refrigerator (at 35–40° F.)	Freezer (at 0° F.)
Fresh meats		
Roasts (beef)	3–5 days	6–12 months
Roasts (pork, veal and lamb)	3–5 days	4–8 months
Steaks (beef)	3–5 days	6–12 months
Chops (lamb)	3–5 days	6–9 months
Chops (pork)	3–5 days	3–4 months
Ground and stew meats	1–2 days	3–4 months
Variety meats (liver, kidney, etc.)	1–2 days	3–4 months
Sausage (pork)	1–2 days	1–2 months
Processed meats		
Bacon	1 week	1 month
Hot dogs	1 week	2 weeks
Ham (whole)	1 week	1–2 months
Ham (half)	5 days	1–2 months
Ham (slices)	3 days	1–2 weeks
Luncheon meats	3–5 days	2 weeks
Sausage (smoked)	1 week	2 weeks
Cooked meats		
Cooked meat and meat dishes	3–4 days	2–3 months
Gravy and meat broth	1–2 days	2–3 months
Fresh poultry		
Chicken and turkey (whole)	1–2 days	12 months
Chicken (pieces)	1–2 days	9 months
Turkey (pieces)	1–2 days	6 months
Duck and goose (whole)	1–2 days	6 months
Giblets	1–2 days	3 months
Cooked poultry		
Pieces (covered with broth)	1–2 days	6 months
Pieces (not covered)	1–2 days	1 month
Cooked poultry dishes	1–2 days	6 months
Fried chicken	1–2 days	4 months

Food	Refrigerator (at 35–40° F.)	Freezer (at 0° F.)
Fresh fish	1–2 days	6–9 months
Commercially frozen fish		
Shrimp and fillets of lean fish	—	3–4 months
Clams (shucked) and cooked fish	—	3 months
Fillets of fatty fish and crab meat	—	2–3 months
Oysters (shucked)	—	1 month
Fresh fruits and vegetables	1 day – 2 weeks (for details, see charts, pp. 29–40)	—
Frozen fruits and vegetables	—	8–12 months
Dairy products		
Milk (whole, skim, 2%)	1 week	—
Cream	1 week	—
Ice cream and other frozen desserts	—	1 month
Cottage cheese	1 week	—
Hard cheeses (like cheddar)	1–2 months	6 months
Soft cheeses (like Brie or cream)	2 weeks	1 month
Cheese spreads	1–2 weeks	—
Butter, margarine	2 weeks	2 months
Eggs (in shell)	1 week	—
Prepared foods		
Breads	5–7 days	2–3 months
Cakes, custard pies	1–2 days	4–9 months
Fruit pies	3–4 days	3–6 months

Source: U.S. Dept. of Agriculture.

▢ Food Substitutions Chart

Food	If You're Out of This Amount:	Use This:
Baking powder, double-acting	1 tsp.	¼ tsp. baking soda plus ½ cup buttermilk (and reduce liquid by ½ cup)
Butter	1 cup	⅞–1 cup lard or shortening plus ½ tsp. salt
Buttermilk, for baking	1 cup	1 cup whole milk plus 1 tbsp. vinegar or lemon juice
Catsup	1 cup	1 8–oz. can tomato sauce plus ½ cup brown sugar and 2 tbsp. vinegar
Chocolate, unsweetened	1 square	3–4 tbsp. cocoa plus 1 tbsp. shortening
Cornstarch	1 tbsp.	2 tbsp. all-purpose flour
Corn syrup	1 cup	1¼ cups sugar plus ¼ cup liquid
Cream, heavy	1 cup	¾ cup milk plus ⅓ cup butter
Eggs	2 egg yolks	1 whole egg
Flour, for thickening	1 tbsp.	½ tbsp. cornstarch
Garlic	1 clove	⅛ tsp. garlic powder
Honey	1 cup	1¼ cups sugar plus ¼ cup liquid

Food Substitutions Chart 🗂

Food	If You're Out of This Amount:	Use This:
Milk	1 cup, whole	½ cup evaporated milk plus ½ cup water
Onion	1 cup, chopped	1 tbsp. instant minced (rehydrated)
Sour cream, for cooking	1 cup	1 tbsp. lemon juice added to enough evaporated milk to make a cup
Tomato sauce	2 cups	¾ cup tomato paste plus 1 cup water
Yogurt	1 cup	1 cup buttermilk

Food Equivalents Chart 🗂

Food	This Amount:	Equals This:
Almonds, whole	1 lb.	1¼ cups
Apples	1 lb. 3 lbs.	3 medium 8 cups, sliced
Bananas	1 lb. (3–4)	2 cups, mashed
Beans Kidney, dry Lima, dry Navy, dry	 1 lb. (1½–2 cups) 1 lb. 1½–2 cups) 1 lb. (1½–2 cups)	 5–6 cups, cooked 5–6 cups, cooked 5–6 cups, cooked
Bread	1 slice, toasted or dried 1 lb. loaf	⅓ cup, crumbs 10 cups, small bread cubes
Butter, margarine	1 oz. 1 stick 1 lb.	2 tbsp. ½ cup 2 cups

🗂 Food Equivalents Chart

Food	This Amount:	Equals This:
Cabbage	1 lb.	3½–4½ cups raw, shredded (or 2 cups, cooked)
Carrots	1 lb.	3 cups, shredded
Celery	1 stalk	⅓ cup, diced
Cheese	¼ lb.	1 cup, shredded
Chocolate	1 square	1 oz.
Cottage cheese	1 lb.	2 cups
Cream, heavy	1 cup	2 cups, whipped
Dates	1 lb.	2½ cups, pitted
Eggs	4–6 whole 8–10 whites 10–14 yolks	1 cup 1 cup 1 cup
Figs	1 lb.	2⅔ cups, chopped

Flour
  Cake
 	
  White
 	
  Whole wheat
	
	1 cup minus 2 tbsp.
	1 lb.
	1 cup plus 2 tbsp.
	1 lb.
	1 lb.
		
		1 cup, sifted
		4½ cups, sifted
		1 cup, sifted
		4 cups, sifted
		3½ cups

Green pepper	1 large	1 cup, diced
Honey	1 lb.	1⅓ cups
Lemon	1 medium	2–3 tbsp. juice; 2 tsp. rind
Mushrooms	½ lb., fresh 6 oz., canned	2½ cups, sliced 1 lb. fresh
Noodles	4 oz.	2–2½ cups, cooked

Food	This Amount:	Equals This:
Onions	1 medium	½ cup, chopped
Peaches	4 medium	2 cups, peeled and sliced
Peanuts	1 lb., shelled	2¼ cups
Pecans, halved	1 lb.	2¼ cups
Potatoes	1 lb. (3 medium)	2 cups, cooked and mashed
Prunes	1 lb.	2¼ cups, pitted
Raisins	1 lb.	2¾ cups
Rice	1 lb. 1 cup, uncooked	2–2½ cups, uncooked 3–4 cups, cooked
Spaghetti	1 lb.	6½ cups, cooked
Sugar Brown (firmly packed) Granulated Powdered	 1 lb. 1 lb. 1 lb.	 2¼ cups 2 cups 3½ cups
Tomatoes	1 lb. 1 8-oz. can 1 8-8 oz. can	3–4 small 1 lb. fresh 1 cup
Walnuts, chopped	1 lb.	¾ cup
Yeast, dry	1 pkg.	1 tbsp.

How to Estimate Servings Needed

Food	Servings per Unit
Meat	
Much bone or gristle	1 or 2 per lb.
Medium amounts of bone	2 or 3 per lb.
Little or no bone	3 or 4 per lb.
Poultry	
Chicken	2 or 3 per lb.
Turkey	2 or 3 per lb.
Duck and goose	2 per lb.
Fish	
Whole	1 or 2 per lb.
Dressed or pan-dressed	2 or 3 per lb.
Portions or steaks	3 per lb.
Fillets	3 or 4 per lb.
Clams	2 per dozen
Crabs	1–2 per lb.
Lobsters	1 per lb.
Oysters	2 per dozen
Scallops	3 per lb.
Shrimp	3 per lb.
Fresh vegetables	
Asparagus	3 or 4 per lb.
Beans, green	5 or 6 per lb.
Beans, lima	2 per lb.
Beets, diced	3 or 4 per lb.
Broccoli	3 or 4 per lb.
Brussel sprouts	4 or 5 per lb.
Cabbage	
Raw, shredded	9 or 10 per lb.
Cooked	4 or 5 per lb.
Carrots	
Raw, diced or shredded	5 or 6 per lb.
Cooked	4 per lb.
Cauliflower	3 per lb.
Celery	
Raw, chopped or diced	5 or 6 per lb.
Cooked	4 per lb.
Kale	5 or 6 per lb.
Okra	4 or 5 per lb.

Food	Servings per Unit
Onions, cooked	3 or 4 per lb.
Parsnips	4 per lb.
Peas	2 per lb.
Potatoes	4 per lb.
Spinach	4 per lb.
Squash, summer	3 or 4 per lb.
Squash, winter	2 or 3 per lb.
Sweet potatoes	3 or 4 per lb.
Tomatoes, raw, sliced or diced	4 per lb.
Frozen vegetables	
Asparagus	2 or 3 per pkg. (9–10 oz.)
Beans, green	3 or 4 per pkg. (9–10 oz.)
Beans, lima	3 or 4 per pkg. (9–10 oz.)
Broccoli	3 per pkg. (9–10 oz.)
Brussel sprouts	3 per pkg. (9–10 oz.)
Cauliflower	3 per pkg. (9–10 oz.)
Corn, whole kernel	3 per pkg. (9–10 oz.)
Kale	2 or 3 per pkg. (9–10 oz.)
Peas	3 per pkg. (9–10 oz.)
Spinach	2 or 3 per pkg. (9–10 oz.)
Canned vegetables	
Most vegetables	3 or 4 per 16-oz. can
Greens, such as kale or spinach	2 or 3 per 16-oz. can
Fresh fruit	
Apples, bananas, peaches, pears, plums	3 or 4 per lb.
Apricots, cherries, grapes	5 or 6 per lb.
Blueberries, raspberries	4 or 5 per pt.
Strawberries	8 or 9 per qt.
Frozen fruit	
Blueberries	3 or 4 per pkg. (10–12 oz.)
Peaches	2 or 3 per pkg. (10–12 oz.)
Raspberries	2 or 3 per pkg. (10–12 oz.)
Strawberries	2 or 3 per pkg. (10–12 oz.)
Canned fruit	
Served with liquid	4 per 16-oz. can
Drained	2 or 3 per 16-oz. can

Source: U.S. Dept. of Agriculture.

Cooking Measurements

Equivalents

Unit	Tsp.	Tbsp.	Fluid Ounce	Cup	Pint	Quart	Gallon
1 tsp.	1	1/3	1/6	—	—	—	—
1 tbsp.	3	1	1/2	1/16	1/32	—	—
1 fluid ounce	6	2	1	1/8	1/16	1/32	—
1 cup	48	16	8	1	1/2	1/4	1/16
1 pint	—	—	16	2	1	1/2	1/8
1 quart	—	—	32	4	2	1	1/4
1 gallon	—	—	—	16	8	4	1

Miscellaneous Measurements

1 jigger = 3 tablespoons (1½ fluid ounces)
1 dash = 6–7 drops (less than 1/8 teaspoon)
8 (dry) quarts = 1 peck
4 pecks = 1 bushel
16 (dry) ounces = 1 pound

Cooking Temperatures

Heat	Temp. (Fahrenheit)
Very slow	250–275°
Slow	300–325°
Moderate	350–375°
Hot	400–425°
Very hot	450–475°
Broil	500–525°

Can Sizes

Can Sizes	Approximate Cups
8 oz.	1
Picnic	1¼
No. 300	1¾
No. 303	2
No. 2	2½
No. 2½	3½

5 Ways to Cook Meat

1. Roast
- Season with salt and pepper.
- Place meat fat side up on rack in open roasting pan.
- Insert meat thermometer into roast so that tip is in center but not touching bone or fat.
- Do not add water. Do not cover. Do not baste.
- Roast in slow oven (300–325° F.).
- Roast to desired degree of doneness. (See chart, pp. 53 – 54.)

2. Broil
- Set oven regulator for broiling. Preheat broiler, if desired.
- Broil meat 2–5″ from heat.
- Broil until top of meat is brown.

- Season with salt and pepper.
- Turn meat and cook until done. (See chart, p. 56.)
- Season and serve at once.

3. Panboil
- Place meat in heavy frying pan.
- Do not add fat or water. Do not cover.
- Cook slowly, turning occasionally.
- Pour fat from pan as it accumulates.
- Brown meat on all sides.
- Season and serve at once.

4. Panfry
- Brown meat on both sides in small amount of fat.
- Season with salt and pepper.

- Do not cover.
- Cook at moderate temperature until done, stirring occasionally.
- Remove from pan and serve at once.

5. Braise
- Brown meat on all sides in fat in heavy utensil.
- Season with salt and pepper.
- Add small amount of liquid.
- Cover tightly.
- Cook at low temperature until tender. (See chart, p. 57.)

Source: National Live Stock and Meat Board.

Kind of Meat	Ready-to-Cook Weight	Oven Temp.	Cooking Time (Min. per Lb.)	Internal Temp. of Meat When Done
Beef				
Standing rib roast	6–8 lbs.	300–325° F.	23–25	140° F. (rare)
	6–8 lbs.	300–325° F.	27–30	160° F. (med.)
	6–8 lbs.	300–325° F.	32–35	170° F. (well)
Boneless rump roast	4–6 lbs.	300–325° F.	25–30	150–170° F.
Rib eye roast	4–6 lbs.	350° F.	18–20	140° F. (rare)
	4–6 lbs.	350° F.	20–22	160° F. (med.)
	4–6 lbs.	350° F.	22–24	170° F. (well)
Veal				
Loin	5 lbs.	300–325° F.	35–40	170° F.
Shoulder	6 lbs.	300–325° F.	25–30	170° F.
Lamb				
Leg	5–9 lbs.	300–325° F.	20–25	140° F. (rare)
	5–9 lbs.	300–325° F.	25–30	160° F. (med.)
	5–9 lbs.	300–325° F.	30–35	170° F. (well)
Crown roast	2¼–4 lbs.	300–325° F.	30–35	140° F. (rare)
	2¼–4 lbs.	300–325° F.	35–40	160° F. (med.)
	2¼–4 lbs.	300–325° F.	40–45	170–180° F. (well)
Shoulder				
Square cut	4–6 lbs.	300–325° F.	25–30	160° F. (med.)
	4–6 lbs.	300–325° F.	30–35	170–180° F. (well)
Boneless	3½–5 lbs.	300–325° F.	30–35	140° F. (rare)
	3½–5 lbs.	300–325° F.	35–40	160° F. (med.)
	3½–5 lbs.	300–325° F.	40–45	170–180° F. (well)
Pork, fresh				
Loin roast				
Center	3–5 lbs.	325–350° F.	30–35	170° F.
Half	5–7 lbs.	325–350° F.	35–40	170° F.
Crown roast	6–10 lbs.	325–350° F.	25–30	170° F.
Arm picnic shoulder				
Bone-in	5–8 lbs.	325–350° F.	30–35	170° F.
Boneless	3–5 lbs.	325–350° F.	35–40	170° F.
Country-style ribs, Spareribs, back-ribs	—	325–350° F.	1½–2 hrs.	—

▢ Roasting Meat

Kind of Meat	Ready-to-Cook Weight	Oven Temp.	Cooking Time (Min. per Lb.)	Internal Temp. of Meat When Done
Pork, smoked				
Ham (fully cooked)				
Whole (boneless)	8–12 lbs.	300–325° F.	15–18	130–140° F.
Whole (bone-in)	14–16 lbs.	300–325° F.	15–18	130–140° F.
Half (boneless)	4–6 lbs.	300–325° F.	18–25	130–140° F.
Half (bone-in)	7–8 lbs.	300–325° F.	18–25	130–140° F.
Portion (boneless)	3–4 lbs.	300–325° F.	27–33	130–140° F.
Ham (cook-before-eating)				
Whole (boneless)	8–12 lbs.	300–325° F.	17–21	160° F.
Whole (bone-in)	14–16 lbs.	300–325° F.	18–20	160° F.
Half (bone-in)	7–8 lbs.	300–325° F.	22–25	160° F.
Portion (bone-in)	3–5 lbs.	300–325° F.	35–40	160° F.

Sources: U.S. Dept. of Agriculture, National Live Stock and Meat Board.

Kind of Poultry	Ready-to-Cook Weight	Roasting Time (at 325° F.)
Chicken		
Broilers, fryers	1½–2½ lbs.	1–2 hrs.
Roasters, stuffed	2½–4½ lbs.	2–3½ hrs.*
Duck	4–6 lbs.	2–3 hrs.
Goose	6–8 lbs.	3–3½ hrs.
	8–12 lbs.	3½–4½ hrs.
Turkey		
Roasters, stuffed	6–8 lbs.	3–3½ hrs.*
	8–12 lbs.	3½–4½ hrs.*
	12–16 lbs.	4½–5½ hrs.*
	16–20 lbs.	5½–6½ hrs.*
	20–24 lbs.	6½–7 hrs.*
Halves, quarters and half breasts	3–8 lbs.	2–3 hrs.
	8–12 lbs.	3–4 hrs.
Boneless roasts	2–10 lbs.	2–4 hrs.

*Unstuffed poultry may take slightly less time.
Source: U.S. Dept. of Agriculture.

▣ Broiling Meat

Kind of Meat	Thickness or Weight	Cooking Time (Min.)
Beef		
Rib, rib eye, top loin steaks	1 in.	15 (rare)–20 (med.)
	1½ in.	25 (rare)–30 (med.)
	2 in.	35 (rare)–45 (med.)
Sirloin, porterhouse steaks	1 in.	20 (rare)–25 (med.)
	1½ in.	30 (rare)–35 (med.)
	2 in.	40 (rare)–45 (med.)
Filet mignon	4–8 oz.	10–15 (rare)–15–20 (med.)
Hamburger	1 in.	15 (rare)–25 (med.)
Lamb		
Rib, loin chops	1½ in.	18
	2 in.	22
Sirloin chops	¾–1 in.	12–14
Cubes for kabobs	1–1½ in.	12–18
	1½–2 in.	18–22
Ground lamb patties	1 in.	18
Pork, fresh		
Rib, loin, blade or sirloin chops	¾–1½ in.	30–45
Shoulder steaks	½–¾ in.	30–45
Country-style ribs, spareribs, backribs	—	1–1½ hrs.
Ground pork patties	½ in.	12–15
Cubes for kabobs	1–1¼ in.	26–32
Pork, smoked		
Ham slice	½ in.	10–12
Canadian bacon	½ in.	6–8

Source: National Live Stock and Meat Board.

Kind of Meat	Weight or Thickness	Cooking Time
Beef		
Pot roast	3–5 lbs.	2½–3½ hrs.
Short ribs	pieces	1½–2½ hrs.
Flank steak	1½–2 lbs.	1½–2½ hrs.
Stuffed steak	½–¾ in.	1½ hrs.
Round steak	¾–1 in.	1–1½ hrs.
Swiss steak	1½–2½ in.	2–3 hrs.
Veal		
Chops	½–¾ in.	45–60 min.
Cubes for stew	1 in.	1½–2 hrs.
Shoulder, rolled	3–5 lbs.	2–2½ hrs.
Steaks (cutlets)	½–¾ in.	45–60 min.
Lamb		
Shoulder chops	¾–1 in.	45–60 min.
Shanks	1 lb.	1½–2 hrs.
Pieces for stew	1½ in.	1½–2 hrs.
Pork, fresh		
Chops	¾–1½ in.	45–60 min.
Country-style ribs, spareribs, backribs	—	1½–2 hrs.
Tenderloin		
Whole	½–1 lb.	45–60 min.
Slices	½ in.	30 min.
Shoulder steaks	¾ in.	45–60 min.
Cubes for stew	1–1¼ in.	45–60 min.

Sources: U.S. Dept. of Agriculture, National Live Stock and Meat Board.

8 Ways to Cook Fish

1. Bake

• Place clean, dressed fish in a greased baking dish.

• To keep moist, brush with seasoned melted fat, a sauce or topping.

• Bake in moderate oven (350°F.) until fish flakes easily with a fork. (See charts, pp. 59–60.)

2. Broil

• Fish to be broiled should be at least 1″ thick.

• Arrange fish in a single layer on a well-greased broiler rack about 3–4″ from heat source.

• Baste fish well with melted fat or oil or a basting sauce before and during broiling.

• Turn thicker servings, such as steaks or whole fish, halfway through cooking time and baste again. (See charts, pp. 59–60.)

3. Charcoal Broil

• Select a barbecue with a closely spaced grill. Grease grill well.

• For smaller fillets, use a special fish grill or barbecue basket.

• Place fish 4″ from hot coals.

• Baste with marinade or barbecue sauce before and during cooking.

• Broil until fish flakes easily with a fork. (See chart, next page.)

4. Deep-fat Fry

• Use only very small fish or fillets.

• Dip fish into seasoned milk or beaten egg and then into crumbs, cornmeal or batter.

• Place a single layer of fish in a wire frying basket.

• In a deep kettle, heat enough fat to 350° F. to float the fish. Do not fill the kettle more than half full.

• Lower basket containing fish gently into kettle to prevent excess bubbling.

• Fry fish until they are lightly browned and flake easily when tested with a fork. (See chart, next page.)

• Drain on absorbent paper.

• Before frying additional fish, be sure fat returns to 350° F.

5. Ovenfry

• Dip fish servings in seasoned milk or beaten egg and then into crumbs, cornmeal or flour.

• Bake in a pre-heated oven until fish flake easily when tested with a fork. (See chart, next page.)

6. Panfry

• Dip clean, dressed small fish into milk or beaten egg and then into cracker crumbs, cornmeal or flour.

• Heat about ⅛″ of fat in the bottom of a heavy fry pan.

• Place breaded fish in a single layer in hot fat.

• Fry fish until lightly browned on each side and fish flake easily when tested with a fork. (See chart, next page.)

7. Poach

• Place a single layer of fish in a wide, shallow pan (like a fry pan).

• Barely cover fish with a liquid such as lightly salted water or milk.

• Bring liquid to a boil, reduce heat and simmer until fish flake easily. (See chart, next page.)

8. Steam

• Use a steam cooker or a deep pot with a tight cover. The pot should be deep enough to hold a wire basket or rack and keep the fish above the liquid.

• Pour about 2″ of seasoned or plain water into the pot.

• Bring water to a rapid boil.

• Place fish on the rack or in the basket.

• Cover pot tightly and steam fish until it flakes easily. (See chart, next page.)

Sources: National Marine Fisheries Service, National Fisheries Inst., Inc.

Method	Market Form	Cooking Temp.	Approx. Cooking Time (Min.)
Baking	Dressed	350° F.	45–60
	Pan-dressed	350° F.	25–30
	Fillets or steaks	350° F.	20–25
	Frozen sticks	400° F.	15–20
Broiling	Pan-dressed	—	10–16 (turning once)
	Fillets or steaks	—	10–15
	Frozen fish sticks	—	10–15
Charcoal broiling	Pan-dressed	Moderate	10–16 (turning once)
	Fillets or steaks	Moderate	10–16 (turning once)
	Frozen fish sticks	Moderate	8–10 (turning once)
Deep-fat frying	Pan-dressed	350° F.	3–5
	Fillets or steaks	350° F.	3–5
Oven-frying	Pan-dressed	500° F.	15–20
	Fillets or steaks	500° F.	10–15
Pan-frying	Pan-dressed	Moderate	8–10 (turning once)
	Fillets or steaks	Moderate	8–10 (turning once)
	Frozen fish sticks	Moderate	8–10 (turning once)
Poaching	Fillets or steaks	Simmer	5–10
Steaming	Fillets or steaks	Boil	5–10

Source: National Marine Fisheries Service.

☐ Cooking Shellfish

Fish	Broiling Time (Min.)	Baking Temp./ Time (Min.)
Clams		
Live	4–5	450° F./10–15
Shucked	4–5	350° F./8–10
Crabs	—	350° F./8–10
Lobsters	12–15	400° F./20–25
Oysters		
Live	4–5	450° F./10–15
Shucked	4–5	350° F./8–10
Scallops	6–8	350° F./20–25
Shrimp	8–10	350° F./20–25

Source: National Marine Fisheries Service.

Vegetable	Steam (Min.)	Boil (Min.)
Artichokes		
French or globe	30–45	30–45
Jerusalem, slices	—	15–30
Asparagus		
Spears	12–16	10–15
Tips	7–10	5–10
Beans		
Lima	25–35	12–20
Green (whole)	20–35	15–30
(French-cut)	15–25	10–20
Beets (whole)	40–60	30–45
Broccoli (split stalks)	15–20	10–15
Brussels sprouts (whole)	15–20	10–20
Cabbage		
Green (quartered)	15	10–15
(shredded)	8–12	3–10
Red (shredded)	10–15	8–12
Carrots		
Whole	20–30	15–20
Sliced, diced	15–25	10–20
Cauliflower		
Whole	25–30	15–25
Flowerets	10–20	8–15
Celery (sliced)	25–30	15–18
Collards	—	10–20
Corn		
On cob	10–15	6–12
Kernels	10–12	6–8

▣ Cooking Fresh Vegetables

Vegetable	Steam (Min.)	Boil (Min.)
Eggplant (sliced)	15–20	10–20
Kale	15	10–15
Okra (sliced)	20	10–15
Onions		
Small (whole)	25–35	15–30
Large (whole)	35–40	20–40
Parsnips		
Whole	30–45	20–40
Quartered	30–40	8–15
Peas	10–20	12–16
Potatoes		
Whole	30–45	25–40
Quartered	20–30	20–25
Rutabaga (diced)	35–40	20–30
Spinach	5–12	3–10
Squash		
Acorn (quartered)	25–40	18–20
Butternut (cubed)	20–35	16–18
Summer (sliced)	15–20	8–15
Sweet potatoes		
Whole	30–35	35–55
Quartered	25–30	15–25
Turnips		
Whole	—	20–30
Sliced	20–25	15–20

Source: U.S. Dept. of Agriculture.

Spice/Herb	Where to Use
Allspice	Baked goods and desserts, especially fruit; sweet potatoes, squash, turnips. Use whole in pickling and marinades. *Tip:* add a dash of ground allspice to cranberry cocktail.
Anise seed	Baked goods, especially cookies and fruit pies; great in orange sauce for chicken, duck.
Basil leaves	Cooked vegetables, poultry, seafood, salads; especially good with any tomato-based dish.
Bay leaves	Soups, stews, casseroles, sauces; use 1 large or 2 small leaves per 6 portions of meat, fowl, fish or seafood. *Tip:* add a few bay leaves to the skewer, alternating them with beef or lamb cubes, when preparing kabobs.
Caraway seed	Cheese dips and spreads, sauerbraten, sauerkraut, pork dishes; good with cabbage, carrots and cheese. *Tip:* add to melted butter for noodles and pasta.
Cardamon seed	Combine with other sweet spices (cloves, nutmeg, cinnamon) for coffee cakes, cookies, buns, pumpkin and apple pies. *Tips:* sprinkle ground cardamon on honeydew melon. Add whole seed to demi-tasse coffee.
Celery seed	Meat loaf, stews, croquettes, salads and dressings. *Tips:* add seeds liberally to cole slaw. Try a dash of ground celery seed in scrambled eggs.
Chervil leaves	Salads, stuffings, sauces, omelets, seafood and cheese dips. *Tip:* mix into canned or frozen peas as they are being heated.

▣ Spice and Herb Chart

Spice/Herb	Where to Use
Chili powder	Chili con-carne, Mexican dishes, cocktail sauces, egg dishes, stews, meatballs, meat loaves.
Chives	Eggs, sour cream-dressed baked potatoes, cottage cheese, cooked vegetables, cocktail dips, creamy sauces, salad dressings. *Tip:* sprinkle over vichyssoise and other cream soups as they are served.
Cinnamon	Baked goods, puddings, sweet sauces, frozen desserts. *Tips:* add some ground cinnamon to mashed sweet potatoes. Use a stick in beef stew or in hot apple cider, Irish coffee or espresso.
Cloves	Baked goods, with fruits or sweet yellow vegetables, ham and pork roasts. *Tips:* poke whole cloves into pork butt. Add to tomato sauce. Add a dash of ground cloves to canned beets.
Coriander seed	Cookies, cakes, biscuits, gingerbread batter, poultry stuffings, mixed green salads.
Cumin seed	Deviled eggs, soups, sauerkraut, pork, cheese dishes.
Dill seed	Sour cream- and mayonnaise-based sauces, dressings and salads. Good with fish, cauliflower, green beans, cabbage, new potatoes. *Tip:* crush seeds and add to homemade potato salad.
Dill weed	Green salads, vegetables, fish and seafood sauces, creamed chicken, marinades for beef or seafood, cottage cheese, egg salad.
Fennel seed	Chicken and seafood sauces, pork dishes, breads, rolls, coffee cakes. Good with celery, sweet vegetables, and apples in any form.

Spice and Herb Chart □

Spice/Herb	Where to Use
Garlic (dehydrated)	Use discreetly in meat, fowl and seafood; salad dressings; soups; sauces; appetizers. Use bravely in Mediterranean dishes—scampi, spaghetti sauces, Italian salads and dressings, bouillabaisse.
Ginger	Gingerbread, spice cakes and cookies. Enhances beef and chicken dishes, sauces and marinades. Use in seasoned flour for frying chicken and liver.
Mace	Called the "pound cake spice," it's also good in cherry pie, light fruit cakes, sweet vegetables, fish sauces, seafood chowders, creamed spinach or chicken.
Marjoram leaves	Roast meats of all kinds, poultry, fish, green vegetables, salads, herbed breads.
Mint	Desserts, teas and drinks; over tossed green salads; with carrots and pickled beets and fruit. Much used with lamb and in Greek cooking.
Mustard seed	*Ground:* cheese dishes, Welsh rarebit, ham salad, creamed vegetables, meat sauces. *Whole seed:* pickling, salad dressings, marinades.
Nutmeg	Cakes, cookies, pies, puddings, eggnog, custards, any lemon dessert. Very good with corn, creamed spinach, chicken, seafood.
Onion (dehydrated)	In meats, poultry, seafood, salads especially. Also vegetables of all kinds, soups, sauces, omelets and egg dishes.
Oregano leaves	Pizza, spaghetti sauce, other Italian dishes. Use with meat, cheese, fish, eggs and in marinades. Ideal with fresh and cooked tomatoes, zucchini, green beans.

⊡ Spice and Herb Chart

Spice/Herb	Where to Use
Paprika	As a garnish and flavor for all kinds of creamed and light-colored foods, like Welsh rarebit, deviled eggs, mayonnaise dressings, white potatoes, cauliflower, salads, dips, canapes, chowders. *Tip:* coat fish steaks lightly with mayonnaise and liberally sprinkle with paprika before broiling.
Parsley	In butter sauces for meats, poultry, fish, vegetables; scrambled eggs; stuffings; soups and chowders; salads and dressings.
Pepper, black	"The world's favorite spice" is good in all kinds of meat, vegetable dishes; even in spice cakes, cookies (pfeffernusse), mincemeat, pumpkin pies.
Pepper, white	Uses comparable to black pepper, but preferred in light-colored foods and sauces, like creamed preparations, chowders, egg and cheese dishes.
Pepper, red	*Ground:* dips, sauces, soups, meats. *Crushed:* Italian-style loaf sandwiches, on pizza and spaghetti, in Mexican dishes.
Rosemary leaves	Roast or broiled lamb, chicken, beef, pork; in sauces for fish, salads, dressings; with eggplant, green beans, summer squash, mushrooms.
Saffron	With rice, chicken and seafood in soups, chowders, casseroles; also in European recipes for cakes and breads. *Tip:* place a pinch in boiling water before adding rice to develop golden color and appetizing flavor.
Sage leaves	In stuffings, meat loaves, pork sausage and pork dishes generally; also in fish chowders. melted cheese dishes, pizza sauce.

Spice/Herb	Where to Use
Savory leaves	With green beans, meat, chicken, dressings, scrambled eggs and omelets; also in soups, salads and sauces.
Sesame seeds	Use in place of finely chopped nutmeats in and on cakes, cookies, cream pies, breads. Good in stuffings, meat loaves, tossed salads, and in butters for vegetables. *Tip:* mix liberally into stuffing for roast turkey.
Tarragon leaves	In salad dressings and sauces for meat, poultry or seafood; also in tartar sauce, egg and tomato dishes. *Tip:* add ground or crumbled leaves to the dressing for chicken salad.
Thyme leaves	With clam chowders, seafood, stuffings, in creamed chicken or chipped beef, and over white onions, eggplant, tomatoes, celery. *Tip:* sprinkle a pinch of crumbled leaves over sliced tomatoes and add oil and vinegar.
Tumeric	Adds saffron-like natural coloring in main dishes that contain rice, chicken, seafood or eggs.

Source: American Spice Trade Assn.

▣ Wine Companion Chart

Food	Wine	Serving Temp.
Appetizers		
Smoked salmon, almonds, olives, hors d'oeuvres, canapes; as an apertif	Champagne, dry sherry, white (dry) port, dry Madeira, white or red vermouth, Mantilla	Well chilled
Oysters	Chablis, Muscadet, Pinot Blanc	Well chilled
Clams	Dry sherry, Pinot Blanc	Well chilled
Soups		
Consomme or turtle soup	Madeira, medium sherry	Room temperature
Heavy vegetable soups, pot-au-feu, oxtail soup	Beaujolais, Pinot Noir	Room temperature
Eggs, pasta		
Omelettes, quiche, egg dishes	Champagne, dry Rhine wines, Moselles	Cold
Pasta dishes with tomato sauce	Chianti, Barbera, Bardolino, Valpolicella	Cool or room temperature
Main dishes		
Barbecue: chicken	Vin Rose; light, dry white wines like Soave, Frascati, California Chablis	Well chilled
Barbecue: beef	Beaujolais, Zinfandel	Cool
Fish, poached or grilled; crab; lobster	White Bordeaux, Fume Blanc, Sauvignon Blanc, light white Burgundy, Pouilly-Fuisse, Pinot Chardonnay, dry Graves, Moselle, Soave, Frascati, Orvieto, Verdicchio	Well chilled
Chicken; rich fish or shellfish dishes; cold fowl or cold meats	Full white, Burgundies, Graves, Rhine wine, Gewurztraminer, California Pinot Chardonnay	Well chilled
Roast turkey	Red Bordeaux, St. Emillion or Pomerol, California Cabernet	Room temperature
Roast ham or pork	Vin Rose or a full German wine like Riesling or Rhine wine; Bordeaux	Well chilled

Food	Wine	Serving Temp.
Main dishes (continued)		
Veal	Light red Bordeaux, Beaujolais, California Cabernet or French Loire wines, California Chablis, Soave, Verdicchio	Cool or room temperature
Lamb	Red Bordeaux, California Cabernet	Room temperature
Beef, pheasant	St. Emilion or Pomerol; light red Burgundy, California Cabernet or Pinot Noir; Italian reds like Barbaresco, Barolo, Chianti Classico Riserva; Bordeaux	Room temperature
Stews, pot roast	Beaujolais, California Zinfandel or Gamay	Cool or room temperature
Game (venison, wild duck); steak	Hearty red Burgundy, Hermitage, Chateauneuf-du-Pape, Pinot Noire, Barolo, Barbaresco	Room temperature
Cheese		
Light cheese	Sauterne	Well chilled
Medium cheese	Cabernet Sauvignon, red Bordeaux	Room temperature
Sharp cheese	Chianti Classico Riserva, Barbaresco, Barolo, Garrinara, Amarone, Pinot Noir	Cool or room temperature
Desserts		
Desserts, pastries, fruit	Sweet Sauternes, Anjou, Spatlese Rhine wines, Champagne, Asti Spumanti	Well chilled
Nuts	Ruby port, sweet Madeira, cream sherry	Room temperature

Source: Italian Wine Center; Haskell's, Minneapolis.

Chapter 3

EATING BETTER

◐ What's a Healthy Diet?

This "New American Diet" gives you suggested daily servings of the basic four food groups. Use it to plan your daily menu.

Anytime: The "anytime" foods should be the backbone of your diet. They are low in fat (less than 30% of a food's calories) and low in sugar and salt. Grain foods are mostly unrefined whole grains and therefore are high in fiber and trace minerals.

In Moderation. The "in moderation" foods contain moderate amounts of either saturated or unsaturated fats. Some items contain large amounts of fat, but mostly monounsaturated or polyunsaturated types.

Now & Then. The "now & then" foods are usually high in saturated fat or very high in sugar, salt or cholesterol.

Food Group	Anytime	In Moderation	Now & Then
Beans, Grains & Nuts *4 or more servings per day*	bread & rolls (whole grain) bulghur dried beans & peas (legumes) lentils oatmeal pasta, whole wheat rice, brown rye bread sprouts whole grain hot & cold cereals whole wheat matzoh	cornbread flour tortilla granola cereals hominy grits macaroni and cheese matzoh nuts, seeds pasta, except whole wheat peanut butter pizza refined, unsweetened cereals refried beans soybeans, tofu waffles or pancakes with syrup white bread and rolls white rice	croissant doughnut (yeast-leavened) presweetened breakfast cereals sticky buns stuffing (made with butter)
Fruits & Vegetables *4 or more servings per day*	all fruits and vegetables except those listed at right applesauce (unsweetened) unsweetened fruit juices unsalted vegetable juices potatoes, white or sweet	avocado cole slaw cranberry sauce (canned) dried fruit french fries fried eggplant (vegetable oil) fruits canned in syrup gazpacho, guacamole glazed carrots potatoes au gratin salted vegetable juices sweeted fruit juices vegetables canned with salt	coconut pickles

What's a Healthy Diet? ◖

Food Group	Anytime	In Moderation	Now & Then
Milk Products *Children: 3–4 servings per day* *Adults: 2 servings per day*	buttermilk made from skim milk low-fat cottage cheese low-fat milk, 1% milkfat low-fat yogurt non-fat dry milk skim milk cheeses skim milk skim milk & banana shake	cocoa made with skim milk cottage cheese, regular, 4% milkfat frozen lowfat yogurt ice milk low-fat milk, 2% milkfat low-fat yogurt, sweetened mozzarella cheese, part-skim type only	· cheesecake cheese fondue cheese souffle eggnog hard cheeses, bleu, brick, camembert, cheddar, muenster, swiss ice cream processed cheeses whole milk whole milk yogurt
Poultry, Fish, Meat & Eggs *2 servings per day*	FISH cod flounder gefilte fish haddock halibut perch pollock rockfish shellfish, except shrimp sole tuna, water-packed EGG PRODUCTS egg whites only POULTRY chicken or turkey broiled, baked or roasted (no skin)	FISH (drained well, if canned) fried fish herring mackerel, canned salmon, pink, canned sardines shrimp tuna, oil-packed POULTRY chicken liver, baked or broiled. (just one!) fried chicken, homemade in vegetable oil chicken or turkey, boiled, baked, or roasted (with skin) RED MEATS (trimmed of all outside fat) flank steak leg or loin of lamb pork shoulder or loin lean round steak or ground round rump roast sirloin steak, lean veal	POULTRY fried chicken, commercially prepared EGG cheese omelet egg yolk or whole egg (about 3 per week) RED MEATS bacon beef liver, fried bologna corned beef ground beef ham, trimmed well hot dogs liverwurst pig's feet salami sausage spareribs untrimmed red meats

Source: Center for Science in the Public Interest. A full-color poster of the "New American Eating Guide" is available for $2.50 from the CSPI, 1755 S St. NW, Washington, DC 20009.

♻ What You Need to Know About the Basic Nutrients

Everybody needs daily or periodic doses of the basic nutrients—protein, carbohydrates, fats, vitamins and minerals. The charts on the following pages identify these nutrients, describe what they do for your body, and list some good food sources. The charts also identify the possible consequences of getting too little or too much of a particular nutrient. If you eat a balanced diet each day, drawing on foods from each of the four basic groups (see previous page), you'll get all the nutrients you need. Large (or mega-) doses of some nutrients, like fat-soluble vitamins, are not only *not* helpful—they may do harm.

Proteins, Carbohydrates and Fats Guide

Nutrient	What It Does	Extreme Effects	Good Food Sources
Protein	• Provides the amino acids necessary for building and maintaining body cells. • Produces hemoglobin in the blood. • Helps make the antibodies used to fight infection. • Is made up of 22 different amino acids, most of which the body can make, but 9 of which need to be eaten in order for the body to get adequate amounts. These nine are called the "essential amino acids."	• **Too little:** Poorly formed or deteriorated muscles, organs and brain tissue; poor teeth, hair and bones; anemia, malnutrition and inability of the blood to clot. • **Too much:** Kidney disease and loss of calcium from the body.	Fish, poultry, meat. Also, non-meat sources such as eggs, milk, cheese or any one of the following combinations: corn and beans; peanut butter and wheat bread; cereal and milk; dried beans or peas with rice, corn or any grain or cereal; nuts or peanuts with grains or rice; seeds with legumes; macaroni and cheese; rice with milk. (See also p. 83.)
Carbo-hydrates	• Provide a major source of energy. • Ensure normal fat metabolism. • Consist of 2 types: starches (complex carbohydrates) and simple sugars. • Many sources provide essential nutrients and dietary fiber (see below).	• **Too little:** Loss of organ or muscle tissue (built of protein) to supply energy, thus causing physical deterioration. • **Too much:** Obesity.	Starches and simple sugars are both found in their most nutritious form in unrefined cereals, whole-grain breads, rice, dried beans, milk, fruits and vegetables. Many refined foods are also sources of starches and simple sugars, but many nutrients and much of the fiber has been processed out of them—as in cookies, candies, cakes, pies, potato chips and other similar snack foods.

Nutrient	What It Does	Extreme Effects	Good Food Sources
Fats	• Serve as the body's most concentrated source of energy and fatty acids. • Provide a protective cushion around vital body organs. • Insulate the body and therefore help control body temperature. • Act as an internal lubricant. • Aid in utilizing fat-soluble vitamins (A, D, E and K).	• **Too little:** Deficiencies in vitamins A, D, E and K. • **Too much:** Obesity, cardiovascular disease, diabetes.	Cooking oils and fats, butter, margarine, salad dressings; bacon, sausage and other fatty meats; cream and most cheeses.
Fiber (not considered an essential nutrient)	• Adds bulk to the diet. • Acts as a laxative.	• **Too little:** Constipation; in some cases, hemorrhoids and even diverticular disease. • **Too much:** Vitamin and mineral deficiency; flatulence.	Whole-grain breads, bran and grain cereals, apples, raw carrots, corn, raw celery, cooked lentils and kidney beans, peas, potatoes, parsnips, leafy vegetables.

Sources: Food and Drug Administration, U.S. Dept. of Agriculture.

◑ Vitamin Guide

Fat-Soluble Vitamins (A, D, E and K): are absorbed into the body with the aid of fats consumed in the diet. These vitamins are stored in the body, so daily doses are not necessary.

Vitamin	What It Does	Extreme Effects	Good Food Sources
Vitamin A	• Aids new cell growth and maintenance of healthy tissues, especially the linings of the mouth, nose, throat, and digestive and urinary tracts. • Is essential for vision in dim light.	• **Too little:** Night blindness, high sensitivity to light and other eye problems; rough, dry skin. • **Too much:** Swelling of feet and ankles, fatigue, weight loss, superficial hemorrhages in the retinae, skin lesions, thinning of the hair.	Liver, dark green leafy vegetables (chard, cress, broccoli, collard), yellow vegetables (carrots, winter squash, pumpkin), apricots, cantaloupe. (See also p. 83.)
Vitamin D	• Aids in the absorption of calcium and phosphorus in bone and teeth formation.	• **Too little:** Rickets, soft bones, bowed legs, poor teeth, bone deformities and multiple fractures. • **Too much:** Loss of appetite, thirst, lethargy, excessive urination, nausea and vomiting, diarrhea and constipation, weight loss, elevated calcium and phosphorus levels, calcium deposits, kidney stones.	Canned and fresh fish (esp. salt water varieties), egg yolk, fortified milk.
Vitamin E	• Prevents oxygen from destroying other substances, such as Vitamin A. • Aids in the formation of red blood cells, muscles and other tissues.	• **Too little:** No clinical effects associated with low intake. • **Too much:** Headache, nausea, giddiness, fatigue, blurred vision, deficiency of Vitamin K.	Vegetable oils, dry beans, eggs, whole grains, liver, fruits, green leafy vegetables.
Vitamin K	• Aids in blood coagulation.	• **Too little:** Hemorrhages and liver injury. • **Too much:** Anemia.	Spinach, lettuce, kale, cabbage, cauliflower, liver, egg yolks.

Water-Soluble Vitamins (the B vitamins and C): are not stored in the body and must be consumed in adequate amounts daily.

Vitamin	What It Does	Extreme Effects	Good Food Sources
Vitamin B$_1$ (Thiamin)	• Aids in normal digestion, growth, fertility, lactation and normal functioning of nerve tissues. • Helps convert sugar and starches to energy.	• **Too little:** Poor appetite, constipation, irritability, insomnia, fatigue, beriberi, swelling of the body (edema), heart problems. • **Too much:** None known.	Whole grains and enriched cereals and breads, dry beans and green peas, fish, pork, lean meats, poultry, liver. (See also p. 83.)
Vitamin B$_2$ (Riboflavin)	• Helps the body obtain energy from carbohydrates and proteins.	• **Too little:** Lip sores and cracks in the corners of the mouth; red, scaly areas around the nose; high sensitivity to light; dimness of vision. • **Too much:** None known.	Milk, cheese, eggs, liver, kidney, mushrooms, green leafy vegetables, lean meats, enriched breads and cereals, dry beans. (See also p. 83.)
Vitamin B$_3$ (Niacin)	• Works with other vitamins to convert carbohydrates into energy. • Helps in the maintenance of all tissue cells.	• **Too little:** Pellegra (swollen, beef-red tongue), loss of appetite, diarrhea, depression, laziness, dermatitis. • **Too much:** High blood sugar, abnormal liver function, gastrointestinal complaints.	Liver, lean meats, peas, dry beans, enriched and whole-grain cereal products. (See also p. 83.)
Vitamin B$_6$	• Aids in the metabolism and synthesis of proteins, fats and carbohydrates. • Assists proper growth and maintenance of body functions.	• **Too little:** Mouth soreness, dizziness, nausea, weight loss. • **Too much:** Dependency on high doses.	Liver, whole-grain cereals, wheat germ, potatoes, red meats, green leafy vegetables, yellow corn.
Vitamin B$_{12}$	• Aids in the development of red blood cells and the functioning of all cells, particularly in the bone marrow, nervous system and intestines.	• **Too little:** Pernicious anemia and, if deficiency is prolonged, a degeneration of the spinal cord. • **Too much:** None known.	Liver, kidney, lean meats, fish, milk, eggs, shellfish.
Folic Acid (Folacin)	• Helps the body manufacture red blood cells. • Helps convert food to energy.	• **Too little:** Anemia, diarrhea, smooth tongue. • **Too much:** None known.	Green leafy vegetables, liver, kidney, navy beans, nuts, oranges, wheat germ.

○ Vitamin Guide

Water-Soluble Vitamins (the B vitamins and C): are not stored in the body and must be consumed in adequate amounts daily.

Vitamin	What It Does	Extreme Effects	Good Food Sources
Pantothenic Acid	• Supports a variety of body functions, including proper growth and maintenance. • Aids in the metabolism of carbohydrates and fats.	• **Too little:** Headache, fatigue, poor muscle coordination, nausea, cramps. • **Too much:** Need for extra thiamin.	Liver, eggs, potatoes, peas, whole grains, peanuts, brewer's yeast.
Biotin	• Helps synthesize fatty acids. • Aids in the metabolism of carbohydrates, fats and protein.	• **Too little:** Mild skin disorders, anemia, depression, loss of appetite, nausea, sleeplessness, muscle pain. • **Too much:** None known.	Egg yolks, milk, meats, liver, kidney, brown rice, lentils, sardines, brewer's yeast.
Vitamin C (Ascorbic Acid)	• Aids in tissue repair, including the healing of wounds. • Assists in the formation of intercellular substances, connective tissue, cartilage, bones, teeth and blood vessels. • Aids in calcium absorption.	• **Too little:** Scurvy (weakness, loss of weight, bleeding gums, irritability); tendency to bruise easily; painful, swollen joints. • **Too much:** Insomnia, high blood pressure, nausea, headache, kidney and bladder stones, dependency on high doses.	Oranges, grapefruit, strawberries, cantaloupe, tomatoes, peppers, potatoes, cabbage, broccoli, brussels sprouts, asparagus, green peas, kale. (See also p. 83.)

Sources: Food and Drug Administration; U.S. Dept. of Agriculture; Dairy, Food and Nutrition Council of Minnesota.

Mineral Guide ⏏

Macrominerals (such as calcium, magnesium, phosphorus, potassium, sodium and sulfur): are found in relatively large amounts in the body. You need fairly high amounts of them in your diet (more than 100 milligrams per day).

Mineral	What It Does	Extreme Effects	Good Food Sources
Calcium	• Works with phosphorus to make hard bones and teeth. • Controls blood clotting and normal response of muscles and nerves.	• **Too little:** Rickets, a decreased rate of growth, and osteoporosis (deteriorated bones). • **Too much:** Calcium deposits in the body, drowsiness.	Milk, cheese, yogurt, ice cream, dark green leafy vegetables (broccoli, spinach, kale, mustard greens, turnip greens), molasses, almonds, dried beans. (See also p. 83).
Magnesium	• Makes proteins in the body, releases muscle energy, builds bones and conducts nerve impulses. • Helps the body adjust to cold temperatures.	• **Too little:** Weakness, insomnia, muscle cramps, twitching and tremors, shakiness, irregular heartbeat. • **Too much:** An imbalance with calcium.	Green leafy vegetables, almonds and cashews, soybeans, seeds, whole grains.
Phosphorus	• Helps develop and maintain strong bones and teeth. • Maintains alkalinity of the blood.	• **Too little:** Rickets, weakness. • **Too much:** An imbalance with calcium, calcium deficiency.	Wheat germ, cheese, mustard, milk, egg yolks, brewer's yeast, dried beans and peas, nuts, whole grains (rye, barley), turkey, codfish, rice, cottage cheese.
Potassium	• Maintains electrolyte and fluid balance in the cells. • Transmits nerve impulses and helps in muscle contractions and the release of energy from foods.	• **Too little:** Laziness, abnormal heart rhythms, weakness, kidney and lung failure. • **Too much:** Abnormal heart rhythms.	Bananas, raisins, seeds (sesame, sunflower, etc.), orange juice, dried fruits, dried beans and peas, potatoes, meats.
Sodium	• Maintains blood volume and the proper amount of pressure in the cells for transmitting nerve impulses.	• **Too little:** An electrolyte imbalance. • **Too much:** High blood pressure and heart disease, kidney disease, stroke, edema (water retention and swelling).	Table salt, nearly all processed foods, olives (green and ripe), sauerkraut, pickles (dill and sweet), hominy, celery, beet greens, chard, soy sauce.
Sulfur	• Promotes healthy skin, hair and nails.	• **Too little:** None known. • **Too much:** None known.	Beets, wheat germ, dried beans and peas, peanuts, clams.

⭕ Mineral Guide

Trace minerals (such as copper, iodine, iron, manganese and zinc): are found in extremely small amounts in the body. You need only tiny amounts of them in your daily diet.

Mineral	What It Does	Extreme Effects	Good Food Sources
Copper	• Helps use and store iron to form hemoglobin for red blood cells.	• **Too little:** Retarded growth, anemia, respiratory problems. • **Too much:** Diarrhea, vomiting.	Plentiful in most unprocessed foods, especially dried beans, nuts, shellfish, organ meats.
Iodine	• Promotes normal functioning of the thyroid gland.	• **Too little:** Goiter. • **Too much:** None known.	Iodized salt, seafood.
Iron	• Makes hemoglobin. • Helps cells get energy from food.	• **Too little:** Anemia. • **Too much:** Toxic levels in the body.	Liver, egg yolks, shellfish, lean meats, green leafy vegetables, peas, dried beans, dried fruits, molasses, whole-grain cereals. (See also p. 83.)
Manganese	• Forms and maintains normal bones and tendons.	• **Too little:** None known. • **Too much:** Blurred speech, tremors.	Plentiful in many foods, especially bran, tea, coffee, nuts, peas, beans.
Zinc	• Helps move carbon dioxide from the tissues to the lungs, where it's exhaled.	• **Too little:** Loss of sense of taste, slow healing of wounds. • **Too much:** Nausea, vomiting, abdominal pain, anemia.	Lean meat, fish, egg yolks, milk.

Sources: Food and Drug Administration, U.S. Dept. of Agriculture.

What Food Labels Tell You

• **Ingredients.** Ingredients must be listed in descending order of prominence by weight. The first ingredients listed are the main ingredients in that product.

• **Color and flavors.** Added colors and flavors do not have to be listed by name, but the use of artificial colors or flavors must be indicated. Artificial color need not be noted for butter, cheese and ice cream, however.

• **Serving content.** For each serving: the serving size; the number of calories per serving; the amount of protein, carbohydrates and fat in a serving; the percentage of the U.S. Recommended Daily Allowance (U.S. RDA) for protein and 7 important vitamins and minerals. (See the following page for a discussion of the U.S. RDAs.)

• **Optional information.** Some labels also contain the following: the percentage of the USRDA for any of 12 additional vitamins and minerals; the amount of saturated and unsaturated fat and cholesterol in a serving; the amount of sodium furnished by a serving; and a breakdown of the kinds of carbohydrates in a serving.

What Food Labels Don't Tell You

• **What standardized foods contain.** Over 350 foods, including common ones like enriched white bread and catsup, are classified as "standardized" (for which the FDA has established guidelines). Manufacturers are not required to list ingredients for these products.

• **How much sugar is in some products.** Sugars and sweeteners come in a variety of forms (white sugar, brown sugar, corn syrup, dextrose, sucrose, maltose, corn sweeteners), and if they're all listed separately, it's nearly impossible to know the true amount of sugar contained in a labeled product.

• **How "natural" a product is.** The FDA's policy on using the word "natural" on a food label is loose. The product may, in fact, be highly processed and full of additives.

• **Specific ingredients that may be harmful.** Since colorings or spices that don't have to be listed by name can cause nausea, dizziness or hives in certain people, people with food or additive allergies don't know which products they need to avoid.

Sources: Food and Drug Administration; *Nutrition Action* (published by the Center for Science in the Public Interest; membership is available to the public for $20.00 per year).

⟡ U.S. Recommended Daily Allowances (U.S. RDAs)

The U.S. RDAs (Table 1) were developed by the Food and Drug Administration for nutrition labeling purposes. They represent 100% of what might be recommended (not required) for a child or adult in most circumstances. However, as you can see from Table 2, not all people need 100% of every nutrient every day; in fact, some need far less, and in special circumstances, like pregnancy, some need more.

Table 1—U.S. RDAs

Protein	65 gm
Vitamin A	5,000 IU
Vitamin C	60 mg
Vitamin B_1 (Thiamin)	1.5 mg
Vitamin B_2 (Riboflavin)	1.7 mg
Vitamin B_3 (Niacin)	20 mg
Calcium	1.0 gm
Iron	18 mg

(gm = gram; IU = International Unit; mg = milligram.)

Table 2—Percentage of the U.S. RDAs (of protein and 7 important vitamins and minerals) for Different Ages and Sexes

Age	Protein	Vitamin A	Vitamin C	Vitamin B_1 (Thiamin)	Vitamin B_2 (Riboflavin)	Vitamin B_3 (Niacin)	Calcium	Iron
Child:								
1–3	35	40	75	50	50	45	80	85
4–6	50	50	75	60	60	55	80	55
7–10	55	70	75	80	80	80	80	55
Male:								
11–14	70	100	85	95	95	90	120	100
15–18	85	100	100	95	100	90	120	100
19–22	85	100	100	100	100	95	80	55
23–50	85	100	100	95	95	90	80	55
51+	85	100	100	80	80	80	80	55
Female:								
11–14	70	80	85	75	75	75	120	100
15–18	70	80	100	75	75	70	120	100
19–22	70	80	100	75	75	70	80	100
23–50	70	80	100	70	70	65	80	100
51+	70	80	100	70	70	65	80	55
Pregnant	+20*	+40*	+20*	+20*	+25*	+10*	+40*	**
Nursing	+30*	+60*	+40*	+20*	+30*	+25*	+40*	**

*To be added to the percentage for the woman of the appropriate age.

**The increased requirement during pregnancy cannot be met by the iron content of habitual American diets; therefore, the use of 30-60 mg. of supplemental iron is recommended. Iron needs during nursing are not substantially different from those of nonpregnant women, but it's recommended that mothers continue supplementing their iron intake for 2-3 months after childbirth to replenish stores depleted by pregnancy.

Sources: Food and Drug Administration; Food and Nutrition Board, National Academy of Sciences, National Research Council (Revised, 1980).

Sources of Important Nutrients 🍎

Below are lists of a few foods that provide significant amounts of 8 of the nutrients for which U.S. Recommended Daily Allowances are available. (See pp. 74–80 for lists of good food sources for the other important nutrients.) The U.S. RDA of protein for a 30–year–old male is 85%. As you can see from the list below, that recommendation can be satisfied with a cup of milk (20%), an ounce of cheddar cheese (15%), and a 3–ounce piece of broiled halibut (50%) or a 3–ounce patty of ground beef (50%).

Food	Amount	% of U.S. RDA
Protein		
Beans, red kidney	1 cup	30
Cheese, cheddar	1 oz.	15
Chicken, broiled	3 oz.	45
Eggs	1 whole	15
Ground beef, broiled	3 oz.	50
Halibut, broiled	3 oz.	50
Milk, whole or skim	1 cup	20
Peanuts, shelled	1 cup	80
Pork chop, lean	3 oz.	60
Vitamin A		
Apricots, dried	1 cup	150
Broccoli, cooked	1 med. stalk	90
Cantaloupe	1 half	180
Carrots, cooked	1 cup	330
Liver, beef	3 oz.	910
Vitamin C		
Broccoli, cooked	1 med. stalk	230
Orange juice, frozen	1 cup	200
Peppers, stuffed	1 med.	120
Strawberries, raw	1 cup	150
Tomatoes, cooked	1 cup	100

Source: U.S. Dept. of Agriculture.

Food	Amount	% of U.S. RDA
Vitamin B$_1$ (Thiamin)		
Beans, navy, cooked	1 cup	20
Ham, diced	1 cup	45
Oatmeal, cooked	1 cup	15
Peanuts	1 cup	30
Pork chop, lean	3 oz.	60
Sunflower seeds	1 cup	190
Vitamin B$_2$ (Riboflavin)		
Cheese, cheddar, shredded	1 cup	30
Cheese, cottage	1 cup	35
Ham, diced	1 cup	20
Liver, beef or calf	3 oz.	210
Mushrooms, raw	1 cup	20
Vitamin B$_3$ (Niacin)		
Chicken, broiled	3 oz.	40
Cod, broiled	3 oz.	15
Ground beef	3 oz.	25
Liver, beef or calf	3 oz.	70
Peanuts	1 cup	120
Peas, green, cooked	1 cup	20
Pork chop, lean	3 oz.	30
Sunflower seeds	1 cup	40
Tuna, canned in water	3 oz.	60
Calcium		
Cabbage, cooked	1 cup	25
Cheese, cottage	1 cup	25
Milk, whole or skim	1 cup	30
Spinach, cooked	1 cup	25
Yogurt, plain	1 cup	30
Iron		
Beans, red kidney	1 cup	25
Clams, canned	1 cup	35
Lobster	1 lb.	20
Pork chops, lean	3 oz.	15
Raisins	1 cup	30
Steak, sirloin, lean	3 oz.	20

⚫ Saturated and Unsaturated Fats

Saturated fats. Found in dairy products, meats and animal fats. Too much can *raise* the amount of cholesterol* in the blood.

Monounsaturated fats. Found in vegetable oils. No unique characteristics.

Polyunsaturated fats. Pressed from various seeds, fruits and nuts (corn, soybean, sunflower, peanut, etc.). May help *lower* the amount of cholesterol* in the blood.

***Cholesterol** is a waxy material produced in the liver and in some of the body's cells. It is used beneficially in many of the body's chemical processes, but too high a blood cholesterol level contributes to the development of hardening of the arteries, the condition that underlies most heart attacks and strokes.

Fat Content
How to calculate the percentage of fat in a product:

1. Locate the number of grams of fat per serving on the label. _____

2. Multiply line 1 by 9 (each gram of fat contains 9 calories). _____

3. Locate the number of calories per serving on the label. _____

4. Divide line 2 by line 3. _____

5. Multiply the result by 100 to get the percentage of fat in the product. _____

The following chart identifies the percentage of saturated, monounsaturated and polyunsaturated fat in various cooking oils, vegetable and animal fats.

Fats and Oils

Food	Total Fat (Percent)	Saturated (Percent)	Unsaturated (Monoun-saturated) (Percent)	(Polyun-saturated) (Percent)
Salad and cooking oils				
Safflower	100	10	13	74
Sunflower	100	11	14	70
Corn	100	13	26	55
Cottonseed	100	23	17	54
Soybean	100	14	25	50
Soybean, specially processed	100	11	29	31
Sesame	100	14	38	42
Peanut	100	18	47	29
Olive	100	11	76	7
Coconut	100	80	5	1
Vegetable fats—shortening	100	23	23	6–23
Margarine, first ingredient on label				
Safflower oil (liquid)—tub	80	11	18	48
Corn oil (liquid)—tub	80	14	26	38
Soybean oil (liquid)—tub	80	15	31	33
Corn oil (liquid)—stick	80	15	33	29
Soybean oil (liquid)—stick	80	15	40	25
Cottonseed or soybean oil (partially hydrogenated)—tub	80	16	52	13
Butter	81	46	27	2
Animal fats				
Poultry	100	30	40	20
Beef, lamb, pork	100	45	44	2–6

Source: U.S. Dept. of Agriculture.

Like other carbohydrates, sugar provides the body with energy. But unlike complex carbohydrates, sugar has no nutritional value. Unfortunately, sugar is not only present where we would normally expect to find it—candy, cakes, pies, desserts—but it's also used in the processing of many other foods—catsup, canned soup, salad dressing, frozen dinners and so on. Sugar, of course, is also plentiful in most breakfast cereals. (See accompanying chart.)

Sugar Content

How to calculate the percentage of sugar in a product:

1. Locate the number of grams of sugar per serving on the label (Listed under "Carbohydrate Information"). _____

2. Multiply line 1 by 4 (each gram of sugar contains 4 calories). _____

3. Locate the number of calories per serving on the label. _____

4. Divide line 2 by line 3. _____

5. Multiply the result by 100 to get the percentage. _____

Breakfast Cereals

Cereal	Percent Sugar
Wheat Germ	0
Granola (without sugar)	0
Cream of Wheat	0
Quaker Oatmeal	0
Quaker Farina	0
Nabisco Shredded Wheat	0
Quaker Oats Puffed Wheat, Rice	0
General Mills Cheerios	4
General Mills Kix	5
Ralston-Purina Rice Chex, Corn Chex	5
Ralston-Purina Wheat Chex	6
Kellogg's Corn Flakes	7
General Mills Post Toasties	7
Kellogg's Special K	7
General Foods Grape Nuts	7
Kellogg's Product 19	11
General Mills Total	11
General Mills Wheaties	11
Kellogg's Rice Krispies	11
General Mills Buckwheat	12
General Foods 40% Bran	13
General Foods Grape Nuts Flakes	13
Quaker Oats Life	14
Kellogg's All-Bran	14
Nabisco Team	14
Kellogg's Raisin Bran	14
Kellogg's 40% Bran	18
Quaker 100 Percent Natural Granola With Brown Sugar and Honey	19
General Foods Fortified Oak Flakes	20
Kellogg's Country Morning Granola With Raisins and Dates	21
Nabisco 100 Percent Bran	21
Quaker Oats Life (cinnamon)	21
Pet Heartland Granola With Coconut	22
General Foods Country Crisp	22
Kellogg's Bran Buds	25
Kellogg's Country Morning	25
C.W. Post Granola, plain	25
Quaker 100 Percent Natural Granola With Apple and Cinnamon	25

Cereal	Percent Sugar
General Mills Nature Valley Granola With Cinnamon and Raisins	25
Pet Heartland Raisin Granola	26
General Foods C. W. Post	28
C. W. Post Raisin Granola	28
Quaker 100 Percent Natural Granola With Raisins and Dates	28
Kellogg's Frosted Mini Wheats	28
General Mills Nature Valley Granola With Fruit and Nuts	29
Kellogg's Cracklin' Bran	29
General Mills Golden Grahams	30
General Mills Cocoa Puffs	33
General Mills Trix	35
General Foods Honeycomb	37
General Foods Alpha Bits	38
General Mills Count Chocula	39
Kellogg's Sugar Pops	39
Kellogg's Frosted Rice	39
Quaker Oats Cap'n Crunch	40
General Mills Crazy Cow (strawberry)	40
Quaker Oats Quisp	40
Kellogg's Sugar Frosted Flakes	41
General Mills Lucky Charms	42
General Foods Fruity Pebbles	43
General Foods Cocoa Pebbles	43
Kellogg's Cocoa Krispies	43
General Foods Super Sugar Crisp	43
General Mills Frankenberry	44
Kellogg's Sugar Corn Pops	46
Kellogg's Sir Grapefellow	46
Kellogg's Baron Von Redberry	46
Kellogg's Corny Snaps	47
General Mills Crazy Cow (chocolate)	47
General Foods Raisin Bran	48
King Vitamin	50
Kellogg's Froot Loops	53
Kellogg's Apple Jacks	56
Kellogg's Sugar Smacks	56

Source: U.S. Dept. of Agriculture.

○ Sodium

Each day your body needs only about as much sodium as you'll find in 1 teaspoon of salt (or sodium chloride), which is 40% sodium and 60% chloride. That amounts to about 2,000 mgs. (or 2 g.) of sodium. Because too much sodium in your diet can contribute to high blood pressure (hypertension), physicians recommend restricting sodium intake, including visible salt and sodium hidden in processed foods.

Salt and Sodium Conversions

To Convert	Do This
Grams to milligrams	Multiply weight in grams by 1,000
Sodium into salt (NaCl) equivalent	Milligrams of sodium content ÷ .40 = milligrams of salt
Salt into sodium	Milligrams of salt ×.40 = milligrams of sodium

Fresh vs. Processed Foods

The following chart illustrates the different amounts of sodium in a representative *selection* of fresh and processed foods. Fresh foods have been prepared without salt.

Beef stew, homemade		Beef stew, canned	
1 cup	91 mgs.	980 mgs.	1 cup
Cheddar cheese, natural		Pasteurized, processed cheese	
1 oz.	176 mgs.	406 mgs.	1 oz.
Corn, fresh, cooked		Corn, canned	
1 cup	Trace	384 mgs.	1 cup
Cucumber, whole		Dill pickle, whole	
1 lg.	18 mgs.	1928 mgs.	1 large
Green beans, fresh, cooked		Green beans, canned	
1 cup	5 mgs.	326 mgs.	1 cup
Hamburger, lean		Hot dog	
3 oz. (1 patty)	57 mgs.	639 mgs.	1 hot dog
Kidney beans, dry, cooked		Kidney beans, canned	
1 cup	4 mgs.	844 mgs.	1 cup
Lemon		Tartar sauce	
1 wedge	1 mg.	182 mgs.	1 tbsp.
Peas, cooked		Peas, canned	
1 cup	2 mgs.	493 mgs.	1 cup
Potato, baked		Au-gratin potatoes	
1 med.	5 mgs.	1095 mgs.	1 cup
Shrimp, raw		Shrimp, canned	
3 oz.	137 mgs.	1955 mgs.	3 oz.
Tomatoes, fresh, boiled		Tomatoes, canned, whole	
1 cup	10 mgs.	390 mgs.	1 cup

Source: U.S. Dept. of Agriculture.

Weight Loss Facts

• The average adult American consumes about 3,200 calories per day.

• 3,500 calories equals one pound.

• 500 fewer calories per day will give you a one-pound-per-week loss. 1000 fewer calories per day will give you a two-pound-per-week loss.

Maintenance Dieting Formulas

To know the number of calories you should eat to maintain your present weight, multiply your weight by

• 12, if you're sedentary,

• 15, if you're moderately active,

• 18, if you're active.

Source: *Successful Dieting Tips,* Bruce Lansky (Meadowbrook Press, 1981).

Calories Burned During Various Activities*

Activity	Calorie Loss Per Hour
Rest and light activity	**50–200**
Lying down or sleeping	80
Sitting	100
Driving an automobile	120
Standing	140
Domestic work	180
Moderate activity	**200–350**
Bicycling (5½ mph)	210
Walking (2½ mph)	210
Gardening	220
Canoeing (2½ mph)	230
Golfing	250
Lawn mowing (power mower)	250
Bowling	270
Lawn mowing (hand mower)	270
Rowboating (2½ mph)	300
Swimming (¼ mph)	300
Walking (3¾ mph)	300
Badminton	350
Horseback riding (trotting)	350
Square dancing	350
Volleyball	350
Roller skating	350
Vigorous activity	**over 350**
Table tennis	360
Ditch digging (hand shovel)	400
Ice skating (10 mph)	400
Wood chopping or sawing	400
Tennis	420
Water skiing	480
Hill climbing (100 ft. per hr.)	490
Skiing (10 mph)	600
Squash and handball	600
Cycling (13 mph)	660
Scull rowing (race)	840
Running (10 mph)	900

*These figures are based on the energy expenditure of a 150–lb. person.

Source: President's Council on Physical Fitness and Sports.

○ Dieting

Men 25 and older   Desirable Weights

Height (with shoes on 1–inch heels)		Weight		
Feet	**Inches**	**Small Frame**	**Medium Frame**	**Large Frame**
5	2	112–120	118–129	126–141
5	3	115–123	121–133	129–144
5	4	118–126	124–136	132–148
5	5	121–129	127–139	135–152
5	6	124–133	130–143	138–156
5	7	128–137	134–147	142–161
5	8	132–141	138–152	147–166
5	9	136–145	142–156	151–170
5	10	140–150	146–160	155–174
5	11	144–154	150–165	159–179
6	0	148–158	154–170	164–184
6	1	152–162	158–175	168–189
6	2	156–167	162–180	173–194
6	3	160–171	167–185	178–199
6	4	164–175	172–190	182–204

Women 25 and older*

Height (with shoes on 2–inch heels)		Weight		
Feet	**Inches**	**Small Frame**	**Medium Frame**	**Large Frame**
4	10	92– 98	96–107	104–119
4	11	94–101	98–110	106–122
5	0	96–104	101–113	109–125
5	1	99–107	104–116	112–128
5	2	102–110	107–119	115–131
5	3	105–113	110–122	118–134
5	4	108–116	113–126	121–138
5	5	111–119	116–130	125–142
5	6	114–123	120–135	129–146
5	7	118–127	124–139	133–150
5	8	122–131	128–143	137–154
5	9	126–135	132–147	141–158
5	10	130–140	136–151	145–163
5	11	134–144	140–155	149–168
6	0	138–148	144–159	153–173

*Women between 18 and 25 should subtract 1 lb. for each year under 25.

Source: Metropolitan Life Insurance Co., Heath and Safety Education Div.

Dairy Products

Food	Amount	Calories
Milk		
Whole	1 cup	160
Skim	1 cup	90
2%	1 cup	145
Buttermilk	1 cup	90
Evaporated, undiluted	½ cup	175
Condensed, sweetened, undiluted	½ cup	490
Cream		
Half-and-half	1 cup	325
	1 tbsp.	20
Sour	1 tbsp.	25
Whipping	1 tbsp.	55
Butter or stick	1 tbsp.	100
margarine	1 pat	35
Cheese		
Natural		
Blue	1 oz.	105
Cheddar	1 oz.	115
Cottage, large or small curd		
creamed	1 cup curd	260
dry	1 cup curd	170
Cream	1 oz.	105
Parmesan, grated	1 oz.	130
Swiss	1 oz.	105
Processed		
American	1 oz.	105
Swiss	1 oz.	100
Milk beverages		
Cocoa, homemade	1 cup	245
Chocolate milkshake	12-oz. container	430
Milk desserts		
Ice cream	1 cup	250
Ice milk	1 cup	200
Yogurt (plain)	1 cup	125

Meat, Poultry, Fish, Eggs, Beans and Nuts

Food	Amount	Calories
Beef		
Pot roast, braised or simmered		
lean and fat	3 oz.	245
lean only	3 oz.	165
Steak, broiled		
sirloin		
lean and fat	3 oz.	330
lean only	3 oz.	175
round		
lean and fat	3 oz.	220
lean only	3 oz.	160
Hamburger patty		
regular ground	3 oz. patty	245
lean ground	3 oz. patty	185
Corned beef, canned	3 oz.	185
Veal		
Cutlet, broiled	3 oz.	185
Roast	3 oz.	230
Lamb		
Loin chop		
lean and fat	3½ oz.	355
lean only	about 2⅓ oz.	120
Leg, roasted		
lean and fat	3 oz.	235
lean only	3 oz.	160
Pork		
Fresh pork		
Chop		
lean and fat	about 2⅔ oz.	305
lean only	2 oz.	150
Roast, loin		
lean and fat	3 oz.	310
lean only	3 oz.	215
Cured		
ham		
lean and fat	3 oz.	245
lean only	3 oz.	160

◐ Calorie Chart

Meat, Poultry, Fish, Eggs, Beans and Nuts (continued)

Food	Amount	Calories
Pork (cont.)		
bacon	2 med. slices	85
bacon, Canadian	1 slice	60
Sausage and luncheon meats		
Bologna sausage	2 oz.	170
Braunschweiger	2 oz.	180
Pork sausage	4 links	250
	2 patties	260
Salami	2 oz.	175
Frankfurter	1 frankfurter	170
Boiled ham	2 oz.	135
Variety meats		
Liver, beef, fried	3 oz.	195
Chicken		
Broiled (no skin)	3 oz.	115
Fried	½ breast	160
	1 thigh	120
	1 drumstick	90
Turkey, roasted		
Light meat (no skin)	3 oz.	150
Dark meat (no skin)	3 oz.	175
Bluefish, baked	3 oz. (1 piece)	135
Clams, shelled, raw	3 oz. (about 4 med. clams)	65
Crabmeat, canned or cooked	3 oz. (½ cup)	80
Fish sticks, breaded, cooked, frozen	3 oz. (3 fish sticks)	150
Haddock, breaded, fried	3 oz. (1 fillet)	140
Ocean perch, breaded, fried	3 oz. (1 piece)	195
Oysters, raw	½ cup (6–10 med. oysters)	80
Salmon		
Broiled or baked	4 oz. (1 steak)	205
Canned (pink)	3 oz.	120

Food	Amount	Calories
Sardines, canned in oil	3 oz. (7 med. sardines)	170
Shrimp, canned	3 oz. (27 med. shrimp)	100
Tuna fish		
Canned in oil	3 oz., drained	170
Canned in water	3 oz., drained	110
Eggs		
Fried	1 lg. egg	100
Hard or soft-cooked	1 lg. egg	80
Scrambled	1 lg. egg	110
Poached	1 lg. egg	80
Dry beans and peas		
Red kidney, canned or cooked	½ cup	110
Lima, cooked	½ cup	130
Baked, canned with pork and tomato sauce	½ cup	155
Nuts		
Almonds, shelled	2 tbsp. (15 nuts)	105
Brazil nuts, shelled	2 tbsp. (4–5 lg. kernels)	115
Cashew nuts, roasted	2 tbsp. (11–12 med. nuts)	100
Coconut, fresh, shredded meat	2 tbsp.	55
Peanuts, shelled, roasted	2 tbsp.	105
Peanut butter	1 tbsp.	95
Pecans, shelled halves	2 tbsp. (10 jumbo or 15 lg. nuts)	95
Walnuts, chopped	2 tbsp.	105

Vegetables

Food	Amount	Calories
Asparagus, cooked	6 med. spears	20
Beans		
Lima, green	½ cup	90
Snap, green, wax or yellow	½ cup	15
Beets, cooked	½ cup	30
Beet greens, cooked	½ cup	15
Broccoli, cooked	½ cup chopped or 3 stalks	25
Brussels sprouts, cooked	½ cup (4 sprouts)	25
Cabbage		
Raw	½ cup	10
Coleslaw, with mayonnaise	½ cup	85
Cooked	½ cup	15
Carrots		
Raw	1 med.	30
Cooked or canned	½ cup	25
Cauliflower, cooked	½ cup	15
Celery		
Raw	3 inner stalks	10
Cooked	½ cup, diced	10
Corn		
On cob, cooked	1 sm. ear	70
Kernels, cooked	½ cup	70
Cream-style	½ cup	105
Cucumbers, raw	6 center slices	5
Eggplant, cooked	½ cup, diced	20
Kale, cooked	½ cup	20
Lettuce, raw	2 lg. leaves	5
	½ cup, shredded	5
	1 wedge, 1/6 of head	10
Mushrooms		
Raw	½ cup	10
Canned	½ cup	20
Okra, cooked	½ cup	30
Onions		
Young, green, raw	2 med.	15
	1 tbsp., chopped	5

Food	Amount	Calories
Mature		
raw	1 tbsp., chopped	5
cooked	½ cup	30
Peas, cooked	½ cup	65
Peppers, green		
Raw	1 ring	trace
	1 tbsp., chopped	trace
Cooked	1 med.	15
Potatoes		
Baked	1 med.	145
Boiled	1 med.	90
Chip	10 chips	115
French-fried	10 pieces	215
Pan-fried from raw	½ cup	230
Hash-browned	½ cup	175
Mashed		
milk added	½ cup	70
Au gratin	½ cup	180
Scalloped (without (cheese)	½ cup	125
Salad		
made with mayonnaise	½ cup	180
Pumpkin, canned	½ cup	40
Radishes, raw	5 med.	5
Rutabagas, cooked	½ cup	30
Spinach		
Raw	½ cup	7
Cooked	½ cup	25
Squash		
Summer, cooked	½ cup	15
Winter		
baked	½ cup, mashed	65
boiled	½ cup, mashed	45
Sweet potatoes		
Baked in skin	1 med.	160
Candied	½ med.	160
Tomatoes		
Raw	1 sm.	20
Cooked or canned	½ cup	30
Tomato juice, canned	½ cup	25
Turnips, cooked	½ cup	20

🍎 Calorie Chart

Fruits

Food	Amount	Calories
Apples, raw	1 med.	80
Apple juice, canned	½ cup	60
Applesauce		
Sweetened	½ cup	115
Unsweetened	½ cup	50
Apricots		
Raw	3	55
Canned		
in water	½ cup	45
in syrup	½ cup	110
Dried, sulfured	10 med. halves	90
Avocados		
California varieties	½ of 10-oz.	190
Florida varieties	½ of 16-oz.	205
Bananas, raw	1 med.	100
Berries		
Blackberries, raw	½ cup	40
Blueberries		
fresh, raw	½ cup	45
frozen, sweetened	½ cup	120
Raspberries		
fresh, red, raw	½ cup	35
frozen, red,		
sweetened	½ cup	120
Strawberries		
fresh, raw	½ cup	30
frozen, sweetened	½ cup	140
Cantaloupe, raw	½ melon	80
Cherries		
Sour		
raw	½ cup	30
canned in water	½ cup	50
Sweet		
raw	½ cup	40
canned		
in water	½ cup	65
in syrup	½ cup	105
Dates, "fresh" and		
dried, pitted, cut	½ cup	245
Figs		
Raw	3 sm.	95

Food	Amount	Calories
Canned in syrup	½ cup	110
Dried	1 lg.	60
Fruit cocktail, canned		
In water	½ cup	55
In syrup	½ cup	95
Grapefruit		
Raw		
white	½ med.	45
pink or red	½ med.	50
Canned		
in water	½ cup	35
in syrup	½ cup	90
Grapefruit juice		
Raw	½ cup	50
Canned, or frozen		
concentrate		
unsweetened	½ cup	50
sweetened	½ cup	65
Grapes, raw	½ cup	50
Grape juice, frozen	½ cup	65
Honeydew melon,		
raw	1 wedge	50
Lemon juice	½ cup	30
	1 tbsp.	5
Oranges, raw	1 med.	65
Orange juice		
Raw	½ cup	55
Canned,		
unsweetened	½ cup	60
Frozen concentrate	½ cup	55
Peaches		
Raw	1 med.	40
	½ cup, sliced	30
Canned		
in water	½ cup	40
in syrup	½ cup	100
Dried, sulfured	10 med. halves	340
Frozen, sweetened	½ cup	110
Pears		
Raw	1 med.	100
Canned		
in water	½ cup	40

Fruits (continued)

Food	Amount	Calories
Pears (cont.)		
Canned		
in syrup	½ cup	95
Pineapple		
Raw	½ cup, diced	40
Canned in syrup		
crushed, tidbits		
or chunks	½ cup	95
sliced	1 lg. slice	80
Canned in its own		
juice	½ cup	50
Pineapple juice,		
canned,		
unsweetened	½ cup	70
Plums		
Raw		
small	5	35
large	1	30
Canned in syrup	½ cup	105
Prunes		
Uncooked, without		
pits	10	260
Cooked		
unsweetened	½ cup	125
sweetened	½ cup	205
Prune juice	½ cup	100
Raisins	½ cup	240
Rhubarb, cooked,		
sweetened	½ cup	190
Tangerines	1 med.	40
Watermelon	1 wedge (4″×8″)	110

Soups

Food	Amount	Calories
Bean with pork	1 cup	170
Beef noodle	1 cup	65
Bouillon, broth,		
and consomme	1 cup	30
Chicken noodle	1 cup	60
Chicken with rice	1 cup	50

Food	Amount	Calories
Clam chowder		
Manhattan	1 cup	80
New England		
(with milk)	1 cup	160
Cream of asparagus		
With water	1 cup	65
With milk	1 cup	145
Cream of chicken		
With water	1 cup	95
With milk	1 cup	180
Cream of mushroom		
With water	1 cup	135
With milk	1 cup	215
Minestrone	1 cup	105
Oyster stew		
With water	1 cup	120
With milk	1 cup	200
Tomato		
With water	1 cup	90
With milk	1 cup	170
Vegetable with		
beef broth	1 cup	80

Fats, Oils and Dressings

Food	Amount	Calories
Cooking fat		
Vegetable	1 tbsp.	110
Lard	1 tbsp.	115
Salad or cooking oil	1 tbsp.	120
Salad dressing		
Regular		
French	1 tbsp.	65
blue cheese	1 tbsp.	75
Italian	1 tbsp.	85
mayonnaise	1 tbsp.	100
salad dressing	1 tbsp.	65
Russian	1 tbsp.	75
Thousand Island	1 tbsp.	80
Low-calorie		
French	1 tbsp.	15
Italian	1 tbsp.	10
Thousand Island	1 tbsp.	25

◯ Calorie Chart

Sugars, Sweets and Desserts

Food	Amount	Calories
Brownies, with nuts	1 piece	100
Cakes		
Angel food	1 piece	120
Fruitcake, dark	1 slice	60
Gingerbread	1 piece	370
Plain cake		
with white icing	1 piece	400
with chocolate		
icing	1 piece	450
cupcake	1	170
Pound	1 slice	150
Candy		
Caramels	3 med.	115
Chocolate creams	2–3	125
Chocolate, milk	1-oz. bar	145
Chocolate, milk,		
with almonds	1-oz. bar	150
Chocolate mints	1–2	115
Fudge, vanilla or		
chocolate		
plain	1 cu. in. piece	85
with nuts	1 cu. in. piece	90
Hard candy	3–4 balls	110
Jellybeans	10 beans	105
Marshmallows	4 marshmallows	90
Peanut brittle	1 oz.	120
Cookies		
Chocolate chip	1	50
Fig bars	1 sm.	50
Sandwich, chocolate		
or vanilla	1	50
Sugar	1	35
Vanilla wafer	1	20
Cranberry sauce,		
canned, sweetened	1 tbsp.	25
Custard, baked	1 cup	300
Gelatin desserts		
Plain	1 cup	140
Fruit added	1 cup	160
Honey, strained or		
extracted	1 tbsp.	65

Food	Amount	Calories
Ice cream, plain	1 cup	250
Ice milk, plain	1 cup	200
Jam, preserves	1 tbsp.	55
Jelly, marmalade	1 tbsp.	50
Molasses, cane, light	1 tbsp.	50
Pies		
Custard		
plain	3½-in. wedge	250
coconut	3½-in. wedge	270
Fruit (except		
strawberry)	3½-wedge	300
Meringue		
chocolate	3½-in. wedge	285
lemon	3½-in. wedge	270
Mince	3½-in. wedge	320
Pecan	3½-in. wedge	430
Pumpkin	3½-in. wedge	240
Raisin	3½-in. wedge	320
Strawberry	3½-in. wedge	185
Pudding		
Cornstarch, vanilla	1 cup	280
Chocolate,		
from mix	1 cup	320
Tapioca cream	1 cup	220
Sherbet	1 cup	260
Sugar		
Brown	1 cup	820
Powdered	1 cup	460
White, granulated	1 tsp.	15
	1 cup	770
Syrup, chocolate		
Thin	1 tbsp.	45
Fudge	1 tbsp.	60
Syrup, maple	1 tbsp.	50

Breads, Cereal, Rice and Noodles

Food	Amount	Calories
Baking powder biscuits		
Home recipe	1	105
Mix	1	90
Bread		
Cracked wheat	1 slice	65
Raisin	1 slice	65
Rye	1 slice	60
White		
soft crumb, regular slice	1 slice	70
firm crumb	1 slice	65
Whole wheat		
soft crumb	1 slice	65
firm crumb	1 slice	60
Crackers		
Cheese	1	15
Graham	4 sm. or 2 med.	55
Oyster	10	35
Rye	2	45
Saltines	4	50
Doughnuts	1	170
Muffins		
Blueberry	1	110
Bran	1	105
Pancakes (griddle cakes)		
Wheat (home recipe or mix)	1 cake	60
Buckwheat (mix)	1 cake	55
Pizza (cheese)	5⅓″ wedge.	155
Pretzels		
Dutch, twisted	1	60
Stick	5 reg. or 10 sm. sticks	10
Rolls (buns)		
Danish pastry, plain	1	275
Hamburger or hot dog	1	120
Hard, round or rectangular	1	155
Plain, pan	1	85

Food	Amount	Calories
Waffles	1	210
Bran flakes (40% bran)	1 oz.	85
Corn flakes	1 oz.	110
Farina, cooked, quick-cooking	¾ cup	80
Macaroni, cooked	¾ cup	115
Noodles, cooked	¾ cup	150
Oats, puffed	1 oz.	115
Oatmeal or rolled oats, cooked	¾ cup	100
Rice, cooked or instant	¾ cup	135
Rice, cereal		
Flakes	1 oz.	110
Puffed	1 oz.	115
Spaghetti, cooked	¾ cup	115
Wheat		
Flakes	1 oz.	100
Puffed	1 oz.	105
Shredded, plain	1 oz.	100
Wheat flour		
Whole wheat	¾ cup	300
All-purpose	¾ cup	315
Wheat germ	1 tbsp.	25

◐ Calorie Chart

Beverages*

Food	Amount	Calories
Alcoholic beverages		
Beer or ale	12 oz.	150
Light beer	12 oz.	95
Brandy and cognac	1 oz.	65
Cordials and liqueurs	1 oz.	110
Gin, rum, vodka, whiskey		
80-proof	1 jigger (1½ oz.)	105
86-proof	1 jigger (1½ oz.)	105
90-proof	1 jigger (1½ oz.)	105
94-proof	1 jigger (1½ oz.)	120
100-proof	1 jigger (1½ oz.)	120
Vermouth		
Dry	1 oz.	35
Sweet	1 oz.	50
Wine		
Table (such as Chablis, claret, Rhine wine, sauterne)	1 wine glass (about 3½ oz.)	85
Dessert (such as muscatel, port, sherry, Tokay)	1 wine glass (about 3½ oz.)	140
Carbonated beverages		
Club soda	12 oz.	0
Cola	12 oz.	135
Fruit-flavored soda	12 oz.	165
Ginger ale	12 oz.	105
Mineral water	12 oz.	0
Quinine water (tonic)	12 oz.	105
Root beer	12 oz.	150
Seltzer	12 oz.	0
Tom Collins mix	12 oz.	165
Fruit drinks		
Apricot nectar	½ cup	70
Cranberry juice cocktail, canned	½ cup	80
Grape drink	½ cup	70
Lemonade, frozen	½ cup	55

*See Dairy Products and Fruits for milk drinks and fruit *juices*.

Food	Amount	Calories
Orange juice-apricot juice drink	½ cup	60
Peach nectar	½ cup	60
Pear nectar	½ cup	65
Pineapple juice-grapefruit juice drink	½ cup	70
Pineapple juice-orange juice drink	½ cup	70

Miscellaneous

Food	Amount	Calories
Barbecue sauce	1 tbsp.	15
	1 cup	230
Bouillon cubes	1 cube	5
Catsup, tomato	1 tbsp.	15
	1 cup	290
Cheese sauce	½ cup	205
Chili sauce	1 tbsp.	15
Gravy	2 tbsp.	35
Mustard, prepared	1 tsp.	5
Olives		
Green	5 sm.	15
Ripe	3 sm.	15
Pickles, cucumber		
Dill	1	15
Sweet	1	20
Popcorn, popped, with oil and salt	1 cup lg. kernels	40
Relish, finely chopped, sweet	1 tbsp.	20
Soy sauce	1 tbsp.	10
Tartar sauce	1 tbsp.	75
White sauce, medium	½ cup	200

Source: U.S. Dept. of Agriculture.

HANDLING EMERGENCIES

97

✚ Emergency Phone Numbers

Police	Pediatrician
Fire Dept.	Dentist
Ambulance	Poison Control Center
Physician	Hospital
Physician	Drug Store
Other	Other

✚ Emergency Supplies

- ☐ Absorbent cotton
- ☐ Activated charcoal (to absorb poison)
- ☐ Adhesive strip bandages, assorted sizes
- ☐ Adhesive tape, ½–1″ wide
- ☐ Ammonia inhalant (for fainting)
- ☐ Butterfly bandages
- ☐ Calamine lotion
- ☐ Children's aspirin (use only as directed by your doctor)
- ☐ Cotton-tipped swabs
- ☐ Drinking cups, paper or plastic
- ☐ Epsom salts (use only as directed by poison prevention center; also for soaking)
- ☐ Flashlight with fresh batteries
- ☐ Hydrogen peroxide
- ☐ Insect sting kit (by prescription only, for allergic persons)
- ☐ Measuring cup
- ☐ Measuring spoons
- ☐ Merthiolate
- ☐ Petroleum jelly
- ☐ Rubbing alcohol
- ☐ Safety pins
- ☐ Sharp needles (to remove splinters; sterilize first)
- ☐ Sharp scissors with rounded ends
- ☐ Snake bite kit (where appropriate)
- ☐ Sterile eye pads
- ☐ Sterile gauze bandages, assorted sizes ½–2″ wide
- ☐ Sterile gauze pads, 2″×4″
- ☐ Syrup of Ipecac (to induce vomiting)
- ☐ Thermometer (rectal for infants)
- ☐ Tongue depressors
- ☐ Triangular bandages, large
- ☐ Tweezers

Source: *The Family Doctor's Health Tips*, Keith Sehnert, M.D. (Meadowbrook Press, 1981).

BONE FRACTURES

Do not move the victim until the suspected fracture site has been splinted, unless he or she is in imminent danger. Note that the treatment of fractures that puncture the skin is different from treatment of fractures that do not.

What to Do

When the skin has not been punctured (closed fracture)

1. Place limb in as natural a position as possible without causing discomfort to the victim.

2. Apply splints. Splints must be long enough to extend well beyond the joints above and below the fracture. Any firm material can be used: board, pole, metal rod or even a thick magazine or thick folded newspapers.

3. Use clothing or other soft material to pad splints to prevent skin injury. Fasten splints with bandage or cloth at a minimum of 3 sites:
- Below joint below break.
- Above joint above break.
- At level of break.

4. Broken bones in the hand or foot can be held steady with a pillow or blanket bound around them.

Where the skin has been punctured (open fracture)

1. Apply a pressure dressing to control bleeding. Place pad—clean handkerchief, clean cloth—over the wound and press firmly with 1 or both hands. If you do not have a pad, close the wound with your hands or fingers. Apply pressure directly over the wound.

2. Hold the pad firmly in place with a strong bandage (neckties, cloth strips).

3. Keep the victim lying down.

4. Apply splints as outlined in procedure for closed fractures, trying to straighten limb and return it to natural position.

Source: "First Aid Guide," © 1978 by the American Medical Assn.

SPRAINS

Care for the injury as a fracture if there is any doubt that the injury is a sprain or strain.

What to Do

1. Place the injured part at rest. Elevate it if possible.

2. Apply cold compresses or ice packs for several hours to prevent swelling. (Do not apply heat in any form for at least 24 hrs. to avoid increasing swelling and pain.)

3. Consult a physician.

Source: "First Aid Guide," © 1978 by the American Medical Assn.

✚ Bleeding, Cuts and Bruises

What to Do
For heavy bleeding

Heavy bleeding comes from wounds to one or more large blood vessels. Such loss of blood can kill the victim in 3–5 min.

1. Place pad (clean handkerchief, clean cloth, etc.) directly over the wound and press firmly with your hand or both hands. If you do not have a bandage, close the wound with your hand or fingers.

2. Apply pressure directly over the wound.

3. Hold the pad firmly in place with a strong bandage (neckties, cloth strips).

4. If possible, raise the bleeding part higher than the rest of the body (unless you suspect bones are broken).

5. Keep the victim lying down.

6. Call a physician or the emergency medical service system.

Additional care for victim

1. Keep the victim warm. Cover with blankets or a coat, and, if no head, neck or back injury is suspected, put something (like newspapers) under the victim. If possible, keep the wound area uncovered so that it can be kept in view.

2. If the victim is conscious, moisten lips and tongue frequently if the victim requests water.

3. If the victim is unconscious or if abdominal injury is suspected, do not give fluids.

4. Do not give the victim alcoholic beverages.

Caution about tourniquets

The use of a tourniquet in instances of bleeding is rarely necessary. Tourniquets sometimes cause more damage in injured extremities and, therefore, are not recommended. However, proper application of a tourniquet may save the life of a victim whose bleeding cannot be controlled in any other way. If a tourniquet must be applied, only those persons who have special training from an advanced first-aid course should do so.

What to Do
For cuts and abrasions

Never put your mouth over a wound. The mouth harbors germs that could infect it. Also, don't allow fingers, used handkerchiefs or other soiled material to touch the wound. Instead, follow this procedure:

1. Immediately cleanse the wound and surrounding skin with soap and warm water, wiping *away* from the wound.

2. Hold a sterile pad firmly over the wound until the bleeding stops. Then change pad, and bandage loosely with a triangular or roller bandage.

3. Replace sterile pad and bandage as necessary to keep them clean and dry.

What to Do
For bruises

1. Apply ice bag and cold compresses.

2. If skin is broken, further treatment is the same as for a cut or abrasion.

Source: "First Aid Guide," © 1978 by the American Medical Assn.

What to Do

If the victim appears unconscious

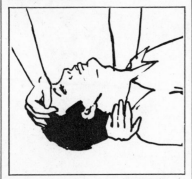

1. Place one hand under the victim's neck and gently lift. At the same time, push down with your other hand on the victim's forehead. This will move the tongue away from the back of the throat to open the airway.

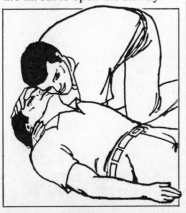

2. While keeping the victim's head tilted backwards in this way, place your cheek and ear close to the victim's mouth and nose. Look for the chest to rise and fall while you listen and feel for the return of air. Check for about 5 seconds.

If the victim is not breathing

1. Maintain the backward head tilt, and prevent air leakage by pinching the victim's nose with your hand that is on the victim's forehead. Open your mouth wide, take a deep breath, and blow into the victim's mouth with 4 quick, but full, breaths, just as fast as you can. When blowing, use only enough time between breaths to lift your head slightly for better inhalation.

2. For an infant, give gentle puffs and blow through the mouth and nose; do not tilt the head back as far as for an adult.

3. If you do not get an air exchange when you blow, it may be helpful to reposition the head and try again.

4. Look, listen, and feel for an air exchange.

If the victim is still not breathing

1. For an adult, change the rate to 1 breath every 5 seconds.

2. For an infant, give 1 gentle puff every 3 seconds.

Mouth-to-nose method
The mouth-to-nose method can be used with the sequence above instead of the mouth-to-mouth method.
1. Maintain the backward head-tilt position with the hand on the victim's forehead.
2. Remove the hand from under the neck and close the victim's mouth.
3. Blow into the victim's nose.
4. Open the victim's mouth for the look, listen and feel step.

Source: American Red Cross poster.

BURNS

What to Do

When a burn occurs

1. Stop the damage. Put out the fire in the fastest way you can. Time is critical. Drop and roll; wrap the victim in a rug; cover the victim with water. Pull off burned clothes. Do not run. (If it's a chemical burn, flood with water and remove clothing.)

2. If a small area is burned, wash with cool water and soap. Do not use ice. Apply a bland ointment like Vaseline® or Noxzema®. Cover with a sterile gauze bandage.

3. If a large area is burned, wrap victim in a clean sheet or towel and go immediately to the nearest hospital emergency room.

Later care of minor burns

1. Clean once or twice a day with soap and water; rinse thoroughly and dry. Cover with a thin layer of bland ointment.

2. Do not break blisters. They provide a sterile cover over the wound. When blisters break, the loose skin should be removed.

3. Watch for any signs of inflammation, redness, pain or swelling. If they occur, see your doctor or go to the nearest emergency room.

Source: National Institute for Burn Medicine, 909 E. Ann St., Ann Arbor, MI 48104.

CHOKING

If a choking victim can cough, speak or breathe, you should *not* interfere. But if the victim cannot cough, speak or breathe, or is cyanotic (blue from lack of oxygen), take action immediately.

What to Do

For a conscious victim

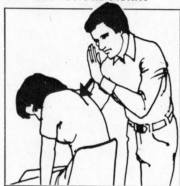

1. Give 4 quick back blows.

• Position yourself at the side and slightly behind the victim.

• Place 1 hand high on the front of the victim's chest for support.

• Lean the victim forward so that his or her head is chest level or lower.

• Deliver 4 sharp blows with the heel of the hand to the victim's spine between the shoulder blades.

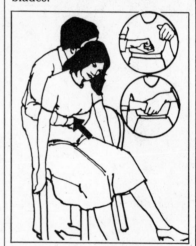

2. Give 4 manual thrusts.

• Stand behind the victim and place your arms around the victim's waist.

• Position the thumb side of 1 of your fists against the middle of the victim's abdomen between the rib cage and the navel.

• Then grasp that fist with your other one.

• Press your fist upward and into the victim's abdominal area with 4 quick upward thrusts.

3. Repeat steps 1 and 2 until effective or until victim becomes unconscious.

CHOKING *(continued)*

For an unconscious victim

1. Try to restore breathing (see p. 101).

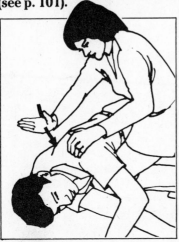

2. Give 4 back blows.

• Roll the victim so that you can position your knees against the victim's chest.

• Proceed with back blows as described above.

3. Give 4 manual thrusts.

• Position victim on his or her back. Straddle the victim's hips or 1 or both thighs.

• Place the heel of 1 hand against the middle of the victim's abdomen between the rib cage and the navel. Place your other hand on top of the first. Your fingers should be pointing toward the victim's chest.

• Move your shoulders directly over the victim's abdomen and press into the victim's abdominal area with 4 quick upward and inward thrusts.

4. Open the victim's mouth with 1 hand and sweep out any obstruction with the index finger of the other.

5. Repeat steps until effective.

Source: American Red Cross poster.

EYE INJURIES

What to Do

For chemical burns

1. Flood the eye with water immediately, continuously and gently, for at least 15 min. Hold head under faucet or pour water into the eye, using any clean container. (Do not use eye cup.) Keep eye open as wide as possible during flooding.

2. Do not bandage the eye

For cuts and punctures

1. Bandage lightly and see a doctor at once.

2. Do not wash out eye with water.

3. Do not try to remove an object stuck in the eye.

For blows to the eye

1. Apply cold compresses immediately, for 15 min. Apply them again each hour as needed to reduce pain and swelling.

2. In case of discoloration or "black eye," which could mean internal damage to the eye, see a doctor.

For specks in the eye

1. Lift the upper eyelid outward and down over the lower lid.

2. Let tears wash out speck or particle.

3. If the speck or particle doesn't wash out, keep eye closed, bandage lightly, and see a doctor.

4. Do not rub the eye.

Source: National Society to Prevent Blindness.

FROSTBITE
Signs

- Skin pink just before frostbite develops; changes to white or grayish-white.
- Initial pain, which quickly subsides.
- Victim feels cold and numb; is usually not aware of frostbite.

What to Do

1. Cover the frostbitten part with a warm hand or woolen material. If fingers or hand are frostbitten, have victim hold hand in armpit, next to body.

2. Bring victim inside as soon as possible.

3. Place frostbitten part in warm water (108° F.).

4. Gently wrap the part in blankets if warm water is not available or is impractical to use.

5. Let circulation reestablish itself naturally. When the part is warmed, encourage the victim to exercise fingers and toes.

6. Give the victim a warm, nonalcoholic drink.

7. Do not rub or cover with snow or ice. Do not use hot water, a hot water bottle or a heat lamp over frostbitten area.

Source: "First Aid Guide," © 1978 by the American Medical Assn.

HEART ATTACK

Learn the signs of a heart attack, and be prepared to respond quickly if you or someone you're with should experience one. (The best preparation is training in CPR, or cardio-pulmonary resuscitation, from the Red Cross or the American Heart Assn.) It's important to know that sharp, stabbing twinges of pain usually are *not* heart attack signs. And you should also know that heart attacks can occur in persons of either sex, even young adults, and not necessarily during physical or emotional stress.

Signs

- An uncomfortable pressure, squeezing, fullness or pain usually located in center of chest behind breastbone.
- Pressure or pain may spread to shoulder, neck and arms. It need not be severe, and it may last 2 min. or longer, or it may come and go.
- May include sweating, nausea, shortness of breath, feeling of weakness.

What to Do
If you experience them

1. Recognize the "signals."

2. Stop activity and sit or lie down.

3. Act at once if pain lasts for 2 min. or more—call the emergency rescue service or go to the nearest hospital emergency room.

If a companion experiences them

1. Act fast. Expect a "denial," but insist on taking prompt action.

2. Call the emergency rescue service or drive the victim to the nearest hospital emergency room that provides emergency cardiac care.

3. Be prepared to give CPR, if you have been trained in the procedure.

Source: American Heart Assn.

Heat Exhaustion/Heat Stroke/Hypothermia ✚

HEAT EXHAUSTION
Signs

- Pale and clammy skin.
- Profuse perspiration and rapid pulse.
- Weakness, headache, nausea.
- Cramps in abdomen or limbs.

What to Do

1. Contact a physician or emergency rescue service.

2. Have victim lie down with his or her head level with, or lower than, his or her body.

3. Move victim into shade or cool place, but protect from chilling.

4. If victim is conscious, give sips of diluted salt water (1 tsp. table salt to 1 qt. water).

HEAT STROKE
Signs

- Flushed hot and dry skin
- Rapid, weak pulse.
- Victim often is unconscious.

What to Do

1. Contact a physician or emergency rescue service. Delay could be fatal.

2. Cool body by spraying or sponging with cold water or by cold applications.

3. Do not give alcoholic beverages in any form.

Source: "First Aid Guide," © 1978 by the American Medical Assn.

HYPOTHERMIA
Signs

- Uncontrollable shivering.
- Vague, slow, slurred speech.
- Memory lapses, incoherence.
- Immobile, fumbling hands.
- Frequent stumbling; lurching gait.
- Drowsiness.
- Apparent exhaustion; inability to get up after a rest.

What to Do

1. Get the victim into dry clothing and into a warm bed or sleeping bag with a "hot" water bottle (which should actually be only warm to the touch, not hot), warm towels, heating pad, or some similar heat source. Build a fire if you're outdoors.

2. Concentrate heat on the head and trunk of the body first—that is, not the arms or legs. Lie on top of victim, if necessary.

3. Keep the head low and the feet up to get warm blood circulating to the head.

4. Give the victim warm drinks.

5. Do not give the victim alcohol, sedatives, tranquilizers or pain relievers. They only slow down body processes even more.

6. Keep the victim quiet. Do not jostle, massage or rub.

7. If symptoms are extreme, call for professional medical assistance immediately.

Source: U.S. Dept. of Energy.

✚ Poisoning

Most poisonings can be prevented if you practice a few safety precautions around the house (see accompanying box). In the event of a poisoning (or suspected poisoning), be prepared to take the following steps. Make sure you've got the number of your local poison control center by your phone.

Signs

- Unconsciousness, confusion or sudden illness when access to poisons is possible.
- Bottles or packages of drugs or poisonous chemicals found open in presence of children.
- Evidence in mouth of eating wild berries or leaves, many of which are poisonous.
- Unusual odor on the breath.

Basic Dos and Don'ts

1. Do have someone call the local poison control center, a physician or emergency rescue service immediately. One person should administer first aid while another calls.

2. Do save and give to the physician or hospital the poison container with its intact label and any remaining contents. The nature of the poison may determine the first-aid measure to use.

3. Do not induce vomiting if the victim

- is unconscious,
- is having convulsions,
- has pain or burning sensation in mouth or throat,
- is known to have swallowed a corrosive poison (see below).

What to Do

If the poison is a corrosive substance (such as toilet-bowl cleaner, acids for personal or household use, silver nitrate, lye, drain cleaner, sodium carbonate, ammonia water, chlorine bleach)

1. Begin mouth-to-mouth breathing if the victim stops breathing (see p. 101).

2. Give milk or water if the victim is conscious, alert and can swallow. Suggested dose: 1–5 yrs., 1–2 cups; 5 yrs. and older, 2–3 cups.

3. Do not use activated charcoal.

If the poison is a noncorrosive substance

1. Give water, 1–2 cups.

2. Physician or poison center may tell you to induce vomiting. If it's available, use 1 oz. (2 tbsp.) of Syrup of Ipecac. For children,

use half of that amount. Follow with at least 1 glass (8 oz.) of water.

3. If you do not have Syrup of Ipecac, induce vomiting by placing handle of spoon or your finger at back of victim's throat.

4. When vomiting begins, keep the victim's face down, with head lower than hips to prevent vomit from entering lungs and causing further damage.

5. Physician may tell you to give victim activated charcoal if you have some on hand. Since activated charcoal may absorb Syrup of Ipecac, it should be given after the victim has vomited.

Source: "First Aid Guide," © 1978 by the American Medical Assn.

106

How to Prevent Accidental Poisonings

☐ **Use safety packaging** when available.

☐ **Keep household products and medicines out of reach** and out of sight of your child. Lock them up when possible.

☐ **Avoid taking medicines in your child's presence.** The child may learn to imitate your action.

☐ **Never make taking medicine a game** or refer to it as candy.

☐ **Store internal medicines** away from other household substances. Properly re-secure the cap and keep the product in the original container. Never store any medicine in a cup or soft-drink bottle.

☐ **If you have a crawling infant,** keep household products stored above the floor level, not beneath the kitchen sink. Never store anything in old soft-drink bottles or food containers. When you use household cleaners, watch your children carefully.

☐ **Always turn on the light** when giving medicines. Never take or give medicines in the dark.

☐ **If you are using a product when called to the door or phone,** take it with you; otherwise, your child could get into it.

Sources: Food and Drug Administration, The Children's Hospital of Philadelphia.

POISON IVY, POISON OAK, POISON SUMAC
Signs

• Itching, redness or blisters on skin after suspected contact.

What to Do

1. Cut clothing from exposed area so that contaminated clothing is not dragged across exposed areas of the body. Use gloves if possible.

2. Wash exposed area thoroughly with soap and water. Repeat lathering and rinsing several times.

3. If blisters occur on skin, see physician.

4. Person treating victim should avoid contact with contamin-ated area and clothing. Wash thoroughly after treating victim.

Source: "First Aid Guide," © 1978 by the American Medical Assn.

SHOCK
Signs

• Cold, clammy skin with beads of perspiration on the forehead and palms; chills; pale skin.
• Nausea or vomiting.
• Shallow, rapid breathing.

What to Do

1. Correct cause of shock, if possible (for example, control bleeding).

2. Keep the victim's airway open. If the victim vomits, turn his or her head to the side so the vomit will not be swallowed.

3. Elevate victim's legs if there are no broken bones. Keep head lower than trunk of the body if possible.

4. Keep the victim comfortable and warm.

5. Give water if victim is conscious and able to swallow. Never give alcoholic beverages, and do not give fluids if abdominal injury is suspected.

6. Reassure victim.

7. Call physician or emergency medical services.

Source: "First Aid Guide," © 1978 by the American Medical Assn.

How to Prevent a Home Fire

Check your house for these 4 sources of fire: heating and cooking, smoking, wiring, and storage.

Heating and cooking

☐ Are space heaters and appliances properly installed and used?

☐ Has the family been cautioned not to use flammable liquids like gasoline to start or freshen a fire (or for cleaning purposes)?

☐ Is the fireplace equipped with a metal fire screen?

☐ Since portable gas and oil heaters and fireplaces use up oxygen as they burn, do you provide proper ventilation when they are in use?

☐ Are all space heaters placed away from traffic, and are children and older persons cautioned to keep their clothing away? Are proper clearances provided from curtains, bedding and furniture?

Smoking

☐ Do you stop members of your household from smoking in bed?

☐ Do you check up after others to see that no butts are lodged in upholstered furniture where they can smolder unseen?

☐ Do you dispose of smoking materials carefully (and not in wastebaskets) and keep large, safe ashtrays wherever people smoke?

☐ Are matches and lighters kept away from small children?

Wiring

☐ Are all electrical cords in the open—not run under rugs, over hooks, or through door openings? Are they checked routinely for wear?

☐ Is the right size fuse used in each socket in the fuse box, and do you replace a fuse with one the same size?

Storage

☐ Children can get burned climbing on the stove to reach an item overhead. Do you store cookies, cereal or other "bait" away from the stove?

☐ Do you keep basement, closets, garage, yard cleared of combustibles like papers, cartons, old furniture, oil-soaked rags?

☐ Are gasoline and other flammable liquids stored in closed containers (never glass jars, discarded bleach bottles or other makeshift containers) and away from heat, sparks and children?

☐ Are old paint–laden brushes disposed of? Is paint kept in tightly closed metal containers?

Source: *Fire in Your Home,* © 1978 by the National Fire Protection Assn., Quincy, MA.

Installing an Early Warning System

Smoke detectors. Smoke detectors form the backbone of the home fire-alarm system. They sound an alarm when they sense an abnormal amount of smoke or invisible combustible gas, so they can give early warning of both smoldering and flaming fires. Smoke detectors are either operated by household current or by batteries. (Batteries must be replaced once a year.)

Installation dos and don'ts

1. Do buy one smoke detector for each sleeping area, and consider additional smoke detectors if you live in a multi-level home. (See next page for suggested locations.)

Suggested Locations for Smoke Detectors

Ranch-style house with two sleeping areas

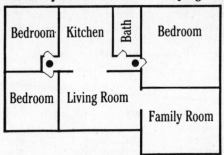

Two-story house

Second floor

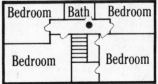

Ranch-style house with basement

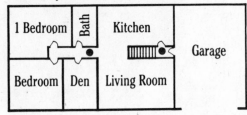

Basement locations

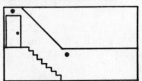

If a smoke detector is located in a basement, it should be in one of these locations.

Split-level house

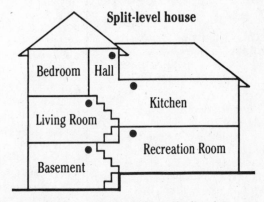

Locate smoke detectors (•) outside each sleeping area and on each additional story of the house.

2. Do locate each smoke detector on the ceiling or high on a wall. Best places
—ceiling: the center; at least 4″ away from any wall; at the highest point of any sloped ceiling
—wall: 4–12″ from the ceiling

3. Don't install a smoke detector in front of air registers or near any cooking appliances.

4. Do test your location before final installation. Make sure every family member can hear it from his or her bedroom with the door closed.

Sources: U.S. Dept. of Housing and Urban Development; *Fire in Your Home*, © 1978 by the National Fire Protection Assn., Quincy, MA.

Planning Fire Escape Routes

1. Make a list of all possible exits from your home. You can't know in advance where a fire will start or how it will spread.

2. Locate two exits from each bedroom. Select a window in each bedroom as an alternate escape route. A window that is painted shut or is blocked by a screwed-on screen is *not* an exit. Be sure that everybody can reach and operate all latches, locks, doors,

bolts and chains. Make sure your children know that breaking a window is a proper and acceptable method of escape. Caution them to remove sharp pieces of glass from the window frame and to cover the sill with a rug or blanket before crawling out. For easier exit from upstairs windows, buy a rope or metal escape ladder.

3. Draw a floor plan of your home. Include all windows, doors and outdoor features in your floor plan. It's important to know if you can climb out on a roof, balcony or garage.

4. Indicate primary and alternate exits from every room on your floor plan.

5. Designate a meeting place outside and mark it on your plan. Choose a spot that everyone will remember, such as a particular tree or the mailbox in the front yard.

6. Locate a fire-alarm box or neighbor's house for calling the fire department. Include this on the floor plan.

7. Go over the entire plan with every member of your family. Walk through the escape plan, taking the family through the escape routes for every room.

8. Train every child in your

home to follow the plan. Children panic in a fire. Often their bodies are found under a bed, in a closet, behind furniture. Teach your children that they can't hide from fire; they must escape it. As early as possible, children must be taught to escape alone.

9. Conduct a fire drill at least once every 6 months. In a real fire you must be prepared to move rapidly and carefully, without panic. Don't warn them of the fire drill in advance. You need to make it as realistic as possible, but don't rush through it too fast. Try to vary the drill by calling out different hazards and different fire sources.

Source: *Fire in Your Home*, © 1978 by the National Fire Protection Assn., Quincy, MA.

Surviving a Fire

1. Sleep with the bedroom doors closed. The closed door offers protection from heat and smoke. Even a lightweight hollow-core door may provide you with extra time to escape by slowing a fire's progress. As you proceed through your escape route, you should close every door behind you.

2. Be sure everyone recognizes the sound of the smoke detector and knows that it means "Get out now!" Just in case, call a warning, such as "Fire! everyone outside!"

3. Never waste time getting dressed or gathering valuables. You don't have time to waste; you can borrow clothing later.

4. Feel every door before you open it. If the door is hot or smoke is coming through the bottom or sides of the door, don't open it. Get out by an alternative exit.

5. If the door is cool and there is no smoke, brace yourself against the door, turn your face away, and open it carefully. Be ready to slam the door shut if the slightest trace of heat or smoke enters the room. A fire that has died down for lack of oxygen could flare up once the door is open. If any smoke or heat does enter the room, slam the door and latch it tight.

6. If nothing happens when you open the door, go ahead and use your primary escape route. Remember to close every door behind you.

7. If the door is unsafe, you will have to use the second choice—probably a window—to escape the fire. If the window is more than two stories from the ground and you don't have an escape ladder, a balcony or other structural aids to use for escape, don't jump. Wait for the fire department. If this happens, open the window a few inches at both the top and the bottom. Stay at the window, keep your head low to get fresh air, and wave a light-colored towel, sheet or some other obvious signal to help fire fighters locate you.

8. If you're on the first or second floor, you can probably drop from your window. It may be helpful to move a chair or some other piece of furniture to the window to make it easier to climb out. Either straddle the window sill or back out of the window, maneuvering so you can slide out on your stomach, feet first. Hold on with both hands to the sill. Let go of the sill and drop to the ground, bending your knees to cushion the landing.

9. Lower small children from the window. There may be someone outside to catch the child and help break the fall. If not, you must lower the child as far as possible. Don't leave the room first and expect young children to follow you. They could panic and you would have no way of helping them out if you were on the ground.

10. If there's smoke, crawl. Get down on your hands and knees. Do not stand up. In a serious fire, superheated air will rise to the ceiling. It may have a temperature of 1,000° F. up there.

11. If your clothes catch on fire, drop to the floor and roll to smother the flames. Be certain that all children and adults in your home know never to run if their clothes catch on fire.

12. Once you are out of the house, go immediately to your meeting place. You have to find out who is still inside so the fire fighters can be informed when they arrive.

13. Call the fire department. Make sure you give your complete address and say if you think someone is trapped in the fire. Don't attempt to call from your home. It's too dangerous.

14. Once you are out, stay out. Never return to a burning building.

15. Don't let anyone go back into the building. Keep a firm hand on small children.

Source: *Fire in Your Home,* © 1978 by the National Fire Protection Assn., Quincy, MA.

How to Fight Common Household Fires

Type of Fire	What to Do
Your own clothing	Don't run—it fans the flames. Lie down; roll over and over; remove the clothing if you can do so without pulling it over your head. Act fast.
Someone else's clothing	Don't let the person run. Get the victim on the ground—grab and push if necessary. Use anything handy to smother the flames—a rug, coat, blanket, drapes, towel, bedspread or jacket. If outside, use sand, dirt, snow or anything else handy. Don't wrap the victim's face—only the body. Try to remove the burning clothing, but don't pull it over the victim's head.
Food in the oven	Close the oven door. Turn off the heat.
Smoke from an electric motor or appliance	Pull the plug or otherwise turn off the electricity. If the appliance is flaming, use water *after* the electricity is off.
Smoke from a television	Keep clear—the picture tube may burst. Call the fire department. Shut off power to the circuit.
Small pan fire on the stove	Cover pan with a lid or plate. Turn off the heat.
Deep-fat fryer	Turn off the heat and cover the fryer with a metal lid if you can approach it. Don't attempt to move the appliance. Don't fight the fire. Evacuate; then call the fire department.

Source: U.S. Dept. of Housing and Urban Development.

What to Do in a Blackout 🔥

You should always have at least a flashlight and a transistor radio in your home. If only your house or apartment is affected, you may simply need to change a fuse or reset a circuit breaker. (See pp. 124–125.) If this isn't the problem, notify the utility company that you are without power, unless it's obvious that a large area is affected. Take the following actions if the blackout appears likely to last any length of time.

Situation	What to Do
Freezer	• Open your refrigerator and freezer as *infrequently* as possible, to preserve the food inside. If the door remains shut, this food should last about 2 days. In hot weather, cover the refrigerator and freezer with blankets or other insulating material.
Phone	• Although the phone will still work, don't use it unless you have to make a truly urgent call.
Appliances	• Turn off or unplug your electrical appliances to avoid damage in case there's a power surge when the electricity comes back on. Once the power has returned, give the system half an hour or so to stabilize before turning on electrical equipment.
Cooking	• If you do any cooking inside your home with a campstove, be sure to ventilate the room adequately. Don't use a barbecue inside.
Emergency Power	• If you need electricity for a true emergency, call the fire department for a generator.

Source: *Just in Case,* John Moir (Chronicle Books, 1980).

⌂ What to Do During a Tornado

Tornado watch: tornadoes and severe thunderstorms are possible.
Tornado warning: a tornado has been detected; take shelter immediately.

Location	What to Do
At home	• Go to the corner of the basement toward the tornado. (Tornadoes typically travel from southwest to northeast.) Take cover under a sturdy workbench or table (but not underneath the location of heavy appliances on the floor above). • If you don't have a basement, take cover under heavy furniture in the center of the house. Keep some windows open away from the tornado. But *stay away* from windows! • Do not remain in a trailer or mobile home. Seek shelter inside the nearest permanent structure, preferably in a basement, underground excavation, or steel-framed or reinforced concrete building.
At work	• In an office building, go to the basement or an inner hallway on a lower floor. Stay away from windows. • In a factory, go to a shelter area or a basement, if there is a basement.
At school	• Go to the basement or an inner hallway on a lower floor. If the building is made of reinforced concrete, stay inside. • Avoid auditoriums, gymnasiums or large areas with poorly supported roofs.
In the open	• Move away from the tornado's path at a right angle. • If there is no time to escape, lie flat in the nearest depression, such as a ditch or ravine. Don't stay in your car if you don't have time to escape.

Source: National Weather Service.

What to Do During a Thunderstorm ⚡

Location	What to Do
Inside	• When a thunderstorm threatens, get inside a home, a large building or an all-metal (not a convertible) automobile. • Do not use the phone, except for emergencies.
Outside	• If you are caught outside, do not stand underneath a natural lightning rod, such as a tall isolated tree or a telephone pole. Keep yourself lower than the nearest highly conductive object, and maintain a safe distance from it. If the object is a tree, twice its height is considered a safe distance. • Get out of, and away from, open water. • Get away from tractors and other metal farm equipment. • Get off of, and away from, motorcycles, scooters, golf carts and bicycles. Put down golf clubs. • Stay away from wire fences, clotheslines, metal pipes, rails and other metallic paths that could carry lightning to you from some distance away. • Avoid standing in small isolated sheds or other small structures in open areas. • In a forest, seek shelter in a low area under a thick growth of small trees. In open areas, go to a low place such as a ravine or valley. Be alert for flash floods. • If you're isolated in a level field or prairie and you feel your hair stand on end—indicating lightning is about to strike—drop to your knees and bend forward putting your hands on your knees. Do not lie flat on the ground. • Persons struck by lightning receive a severe electrical shock and may be burned, but they carry no electrical charge and can be handled safely. If a victim is not breathing, first aid should be given within 4–6 minutes or less to prevent irrevocable damage to the brain. (See p. 101.) If the victim has no pulse, a qualified person should administer CPR (cardiopulmonary resuscitation).

Source: National Weather Service.

⚙ What to Do During a Hurricane

Time	What to Do
When a hurricane *watch* is issued for your area	• Keep listening for official bulletins on radio and TV. • Fuel your car. • Check mobile home tie-downs. • Moor small craft or move to safe shelter. • Stock up on canned food. • Check supplies of special medicines and drugs. • Check batteries for radio and flashlights. • Secure lawn furniture and other loose material outdoors. • Tape, board or shutter windows to prevent shattering. • Wedge sliding glass doors to keep them from lifting out of their tracks.
When a hurricane *warning* is issued for your area	• Stay tuned to radio or TV for official bulletins. • Stay home if it's sturdy and on high ground. Board up garage and porch doors; move valuables to upper floors; bring in pets; fill containers (including the bathtub) with several days' supply of drinking water; turn up the refrigerator to maximum cold and don't open unless necessary; use phone only for emergencies; and stay indoors on the downwind side of the house, away from windows. • Leave mobile homes. • Leave areas that might be affected by storm tide or stream flooding. Leave early, in daylight if possible; shut off water and electricity at main stations; take small valuables and papers, but travel light; leave food and water for pets (shelters will not take them in); lock up your house; and drive carefully to the nearest designated shelter using recommended evacuation routes.
After the all-clear is given	• Drive carefully; watch for dangling electrical wires, undermined roads, flooded low spots. • Report broken or damaged water, sewer and electrical lines. • Use caution when re-entering your home—check for gas leaks; check food and water for spoilage.

Source: National Weather Service.

What to Do in an Earthquake 🔥

Time	What to Do
During an earthquake	• Stay where you are. If outdoors, stay outdoors. If indoors, stay indoors. Most injuries occur as people are entering or leaving buildings. • If you *are* indoors, take cover under a desk, table, bench or against inside walls or doorways. Stay away from glass, windows and outside doors. • If you're outside, move away from buildings and utility wires. Once you're in the open, stay there until the shaking stops. • Don't run through or near buildings. The greatest danger from falling debris is just outside doorways and close to outer walls. • If you're in a moving car, stop as quickly as safety permits, but stay in the vehicle. When you drive on, watch for hazards created by the earthquake, such as fallen or falling objects, downed electrical wires, or broken or undermined roadways.
After an earthquake	• Check for injuries. Do not attempt to move seriously injured persons unless they are in immediate danger of further injury. • Check utility lines and appliances for damage. If you smell gas, open windows and shut off the main gas valve. Then leave the building and report gas leakage to authorities. Don't re-enter the building until a utility official says it is safe. • If water pipes are damaged, shut off the supply of the main valve. Emergency water may be obtained from such sources as hot water tanks, toilet tanks and even melted ice cubes! • Check to see that sewage lines are intact before toilets are flushed. • If electrical wiring is shorting out, shut off current at the main meter box. • Check chimneys for cracks and damage. Unnoticed damage could lead to fire. The initial check should be made from a distance; approach chimneys with great caution. • Stay off the phone, except to report an emergency.

Source: Office of Public Affairs, Federal Emergency Management Agency.

Chapter 5

MAINTAINING YOUR HOME

⛏ Emergency Phone Numbers

Electrician	Gas Co.
Exterminator	Plumber
Furnace Repair	Water Co.
Electric Co.	Other

⛏ Tool Box Checklist

- ☐ 3 screwdrivers (with $\frac{3}{16}''$, $\frac{1}{4}''$ and $\frac{5}{16}''$ blades)
- ☐ 2 Phillips screwdrivers (a #1 and a #2)
- ☐ 1 claw hammer (12– or 13–oz.)
- ☐ 1 pliers (7")
- ☐ 1 vise-grip pliers
- ☐ 1 needlenose pliers
- ☐ 1 adjustable wrench (10" or larger)
- ☐ 1 level (6–12")
- ☐ 1 steel square (8"-by-12")
- ☐ 1 cross-cut handsaw (with 8–10 teeth points per inch)
- ☐ 1 tape measure (12')
- ☐ 1–2 putty knives (2 widths)
- ☐ 4–5 wood chisels (from $\frac{1}{4}''$–1" wide)
- ☐ 1 hacksaw
- ☐ 1 center punch ($\frac{3}{8}''$-by-4")
- ☐ 1 electric drill (with 5–7 drill bits up to $\frac{1}{4}''$ in diameter)
- ☐ sandpaper (various grades)
- ☐ 1 rubber drain plunger
- ☐ C–clamps
- ☐ masking and black electrical tape
- ☐ white polyvinyl glue
- ☐ 1 can light machine or household oil
- ☐ nails, screws

Source: U.S. Dept. of Agriculture.

Troubleshooting Chart for Electrical Appliances 🔧

Before you call in a professional to repair an appliance that won't work, see if you can make the repair yourself. It's *possible* that something quite simple is keeping your appliance from working. The Association of Home Appliance Manufacturers estimates that about 40% of all service calls are unwarranted. Save yourself some unnecessary repair bills by first running through the following checklist for *all* appliances. Then check the chart on this and the following 2 pages for the *specific* appliance you're trying to fix. If none of these procedures work, then call in a professional.

What to Check First

☐ **Is the switch on?**

☐ **Is the plug firmly inserted into the wall outlet?** You can bend the prongs slightly outward with a pair of pliers to make them fit. Or you can clean the prongs with sandpaper.

☐ **Is the cord in good shape?** Replace if necessary. (Note that on some appliances, servicemen should handle cord replacement. Check manufacturer's instructions.)

☐ **Has the fuse or circuit breaker in the appliance blown?**

☐ **Has the wall outlet gone dead?** Check by plugging in a lamp you know is working.

☐ **Has there been an overload?** All major motor-driven appliances—clothes washers, dryers and so on—have an "overload protector" that will turn off the power to the appliance if there's an overload or if the motor becomes overheated. After the overload has been removed or the motor has cooled down, reset the switch. (Some reset automatically.)

☐ **Has there been a power failure?** Check other circuits or see if your neighbors have power. (See p. 113 for what to do during a blackout.)

What to Check Second

Appliance	Problem	Possible Cause	Remedy
Oven	Won't heat.	• Timer set at "off" or "automatic" position.	Reset timer to "manual."
		• Selector switch in wrong position.	• Set selector switch to "bake."
Refrigerator, freezer	Won't operate.	• Temperature control set at "off" or "defrost."	• If model defrosts manually, turn "on." If model defrosts automatically, check manufacturer's instructions on timing of defrost cycle.
		• Use of long extension cord, smaller than No. 14 wire.	• Extension cords of any kind should not be used. If there's no alternative, use a 3-wire, No. 14 (or heavier) cord.

⊞ Troubleshooting Chart for Electrical Appliances

Appliance	Problem	Possible Cause	Remedy
Refrigerator, freezer	Motor runs too often, too long.	• Dust on condenser.	• Turn off or disconnect appliance. Clean condenser according to manufacturer's instructions.
		• Door leaking air. Check by first closing door over dollar bill and then pulling bill out. If it pulls out easily, it's leaking air.	• Clean door gasket with soap and water. Have replaced if torn or worn. Also, you may need to adjust the latch.
		• Unit too near a heat source or too close to wall or cabinets.	• Move unit to a different location.
Refrigerator, freezer	Food slow to freeze.	• Freezing too much food at one time.	• Freeze no more than 2–3 lbs. of food per cubic foot of freezer space in a 24-hr. period.
		• Too much frost.	• Defrost before ice becomes ¼" thick.
Dishwasher	Won't operate.	• Door latch not completely closed.	• Reclose door and latch securely.
		• Cycle control not on proper setting.	• Adjust control, following manufacturer's instructions.
Dishwasher	Dishes not clean.	• Water not hot enough.	• Water heater should be set to 150°.
		• Dishes/cutlery not properly prepared or loaded.	• Scrape dishes. Follow manufacturer's loading instructions.
		• Dishwasher drain clogged.	• Clean drain and strainer according to manufacturer's instructions.
Clothes washer	Water doesn't run into washer.	• Faucets not open.	• Check faucets.
		• Kink in hose.	• Straighten.
		• Screens stopped up.	• Remove hose at faucets and washer. Clean screens.
Clothes washer	Water doesn't drain from washer.	• Kink in discharge hose.	• Straighten hose.
Clothes dryer	Does not operate.	• Door not firmly closed.	• Reclose door firmly.
		• Controls not properly set.	• Check position of controls and adjust to proper setting.

Troubleshooting Chart for Electrical Appliances 🔌

Appliance	Problem	Possible Cause	Remedy
Clothes dryer	Clothes don't dry in proper time.	• Dryer overloaded.	• Follow manufacturer's instructions for loading.
		• Lint tray full.	• Clean. Empty after each use.
Room air conditioner	Fuse or circuit breaker frequently blows.	• Circuit overloaded.	• Remove other electrical equipment from air-conditioning circuit, or have special circuit installed for unit.
Room air conditioner	Unit operates; room not cool enough.	• Dirty filter in unit.	• Clean or replace filter.
		• Bushes or other obstruction interfering with outdoor air flow.	• Trim bushes; remove any other obstruction to at least 1' away.
		• Too much heat build-up before unit is started.	• Turn unit on earlier. Keep shades drawn, windows and doors closed to reduce heat load.
		• Heat or hot-water vapor from kitchen or bathroom coming into room.	• Release heat or vapor through windows in kitchen or bedroom, preferably with exhaust fan.
		• Round-the-clock use can cause ice to build on coils and block air flow.	• Turn unit off until ice melts.

Source: Edison Electric Inst.

🔧 How to Replace a Fuse/Reset a Circuit Breaker

The circuits in your home are protected by either fuses or circuit breakers. A fuse will blow or a circuit breaker will trip off when the circuit it protects is overloaded or interrupted. It's very easy to replace a fuse or reset a circuit breaker (see chart on the next page), but unless you discover the cause of the problem, you'll blow the fuse or trip the breaker again. The chart below identifies 3 typical problems and remedies.

Problem/Symptom	Remedy
Problem: Overloaded circuit. **Symptom:** Metal strip inside fuse is broken; or circuit breaker is tripped off.	1. Add up the wattages of all lights and appliances on each circuit. Wattages are shown on light bulbs and on the nameplates of all appliances. (You can also use the table on the next page to make an estimate.) 2. If the wattage of the lights and appliances in use at the same time exceeds 1800 watts for a 15–amp circuit or 2400 watts for a 20–amp circuit, the circuit is overloaded. (The fuse or the breaker box will tell you what kind of circuit you have.) 3. Turn off some of the appliances before you restore power.
Problem: Temporary overload. **Symptom:** Fuse blows when a motor starts.	1. Install dual-element time-delay fuses which are designed to handle the extra power, but will blow when there's a real overload.
Problem: Short circuit. **Symptom:** Metal strip inside fuse is blackened or discolored; or circuit breaker is tripped off.	1. Turn off all lights and unplug all appliances on the circuit. Replace fuse or reset circuit breaker. If fuse still blows (or circuit breaker trips), the trouble is in the wiring, a switch, receptacle or other built-in device. A qualified electrician is needed. 2. Check all plugs for evidence of burning or sparking (black marks or burns), which indicates that a short occurred in the plug. Replace plug (see p. 126). 3. If trouble is still not found, turn on lights and plug in appliances one by one. When defective device is found, disconnect it until it's replaced or repaired.

Source: U.S. Dept of Housing and Urban Development

Typical Wattages of Home Appliances

Appliance	Typical Wattage
Mixer, window fan, television, (black-and-white), humidifier, electric blanket	100–200 watts
Blender, trash compactor, dehumidifier, television (color), floor polisher	200–400 watts
Garbage disposal, hair dryer, vacuum cleaner	400–600 watts
Broiler, coffee maker, deep fryer, frying pan, dishwasher, hot plate, microwave oven, toaster, waffle iron, portable heater, iron	1,000–1,500 watts

Source: Edison Electric Inst.

How to Restore Power

	How to Identify What to Replace/Reset	How to Replace/Reset
Fuse *Plug fuse Time-delay fuse Breaker fuse*	• The metal strip inside blown fuse is either broken or blackened, or the spring-loaded metal strip on a time-delay fuse has broken. • The reset button on breaker-type fuse has popped out.	• Unscrew blown fuse* and replace it with one of the same capacity. Never, for instance, replace a 15-amp fuse with a larger one. And never use a penny as a replacement. You could start a fire. • Push button in to reset.
Circuit	• The breaker switch is at the "tripped" or "off" position. Often a red stripe will appear.	• Push switch to "off" and then "on" or "reset" position.

*****Caution:** Never stand in water when changing fuses. It's best to wear rubber sneakers, stand on a rubber mat or wooden boards, and wear gloves when replacing a fuse. If the fuse can't be easily removed, do *not* try to use a pliers or screwdriver to aid you. Call an electrician.

⚏ How to Replace an Electric Plug

Electric plugs rarely wear out, but it's quite common for a lamp or appliance cord to crack or for wires to become exposed near the plug. In either case, you'll need to cut part of the cord off and replace the plug. Here's how:

Supplies

- new plug
- screwdriver
- needlenose pliers

What to Do

For round-wire plugs

1. Cut off the cord at the damaged part or close to the plug you're replacing.

2. Slip the new plug on to the cord.

3. Clip away the outer insulation, revealing the two wires beneath it.

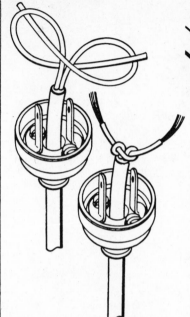

4. Tie an underwriters' knot.

5. Remove 1″ of the insulation from the end of each of the 2 wires. Do not cut any of the small wires.

6. Twist small wires together, clockwise. If the wires are solid, bend them into a small hook.

7. Pull knot down firmly in the plug.

8. Wrap one wire around each pole or screw, clockwise (i.e., in the direction the screw will tighten).

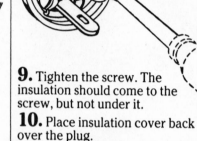

9. Tighten the screw. The insulation should come to the screw, but not under it.

10. Place insulation cover back over the plug.

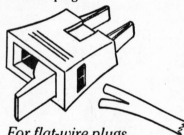

For flat-wire plugs

1. Open the clamp on top.

2. Cut off the end of the cord so that no copper wires stick out.

3. Slit cord about ¼″.

4. Slip it in the side of the plug as far as it will go.

5. Close the top clamp.

Source: U.S. Dept. of Agriculture.

Compression faucets have separate handles for hot and cold water. If one of them leaks, it's usually the washer that needs replacing. Follow the procedure described below. *(Noncompression*—or washerless—faucets have a single handle that controls both the hot and cold water. If it leaks, you generally have to replace the whole faucet.)

Supplies

- wrench
- screwdriver
- new washer

What to Do

1. Shut off the water supply. Usually there's a shut-off valve under the sink, but if there isn't one, shut off the branch-line valve in the basement or the main valve where the water supply enters the house. Then turn on the faucet until the water stops flowing.

2. Unscrew and remove the faucet handle. You'll often have to first pry off the decorative cap that hides the screw.

3. Using a smooth-jawed wrench that you've padded with cloth, unscrew the large packing nut and pull out the faucet stem. Then remove the screw from

the bottom of the stem and pry out the worn washer. If the screw is tight or stubborn, tap its head slightly or apply kerosene.

4. Clean out the washer seat and insert the new washer. (It should be of the same size and composition as the one it's replacing.) The new washer should fit snugly without having to be forced into position. After

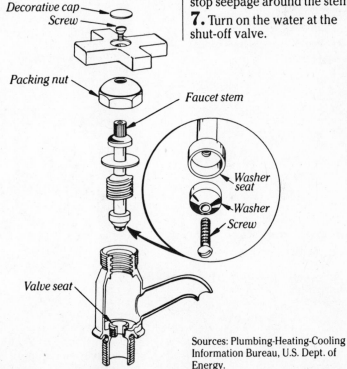

Decorative cap
Screw

Packing nut

Faucet stem

Washer seat

Washer

Screw

Valve seat

inserting it, replace and tighten the screw.

5. While you have the faucet stem out, use a cloth to clean the valve seat inside the faucet. The edge should be smooth and free from nicks; if it's not, you may have to have it replaced.

6. Replace the faucet stem and tighten the packing nut. Tighten it only as much as necessary to stop seepage around the stem.

7. Turn on the water at the shut-off valve.

Sources: Plumbing-Heating-Cooling Information Bureau, U.S. Dept. of Energy.

🔧 How to Unclog a Sink or Toilet

UNCLOGGING A SINK

Sink stoppages in the kitchen are usually caused by liquid fats and other wastes that hit the cooler pipe and solidify. Coffee grounds and bits of food add to this layer until the pipe becomes impassable. To prevent this, pour excess grease into a tin can and throw it out with the garbage, not down the sink drain. To unclog a drain, try these methods, in order, until your drain is clear.

Supplies

- screwdriver
- bathroom plunger
- household ammonia
- boiling water
- wrench
- cloth or adhesive tape
- wire hanger
- auger, or "snake" (can be rented)
- rubber gloves

What to Do

1. Remove the perforated drain plate or strainer in the sink basin; sometimes the stoppage is directly below this and can be loosened with a long screwdriver or a piece of wire.

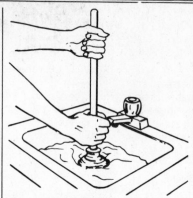

2. Cup your plunger tightly over the drain, and plunge it vigorously several times after pouring a teakettle of boiling water into the drain to help soften whatever is clogging the pipe. Follow with a little household ammonia.

3. Unscrew the cleanout plug at the bottom of the U-trap below the sink. If there is no cleanout plug, remove the whole U-trap, first placing adhesive tape or cloth around the nuts so that the wrench jaw won't scratch the chrome surface. Put a bucket directly under the pipe to catch anything that drips out. Pull out the clogging material with a piece of wire or a bent coat-hanger. Replace the trap and run hot water through the system to flush it out.

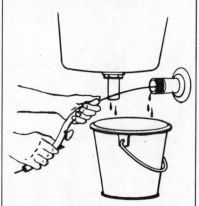

4. Use an auger (often called a "snake") to drill through a clog that's farther down the pipe. An auger, which you can rent if you don't own one, has an adjustable, crank-type handle that you turn to uncoil a spring-steel or coiled wire. Feed the wire into the pipe below the U-trap, which must be removed. Gently uncoil the

UNCLOGGING A SINK
(continued)

snake until it stops, and then move it back and forth until you've broken through the clogged area. Remove the auger, replace the trap, and run hot water through the system. *Caution:* if you've used any drain cleaners, be sure to wear rubber gloves when trying any of these methods. These cleaners can cause severe burns on hands and arms.

Source: Plumbing-Heating-Cooling Information Bureau.

UNCLOGGING A TOILET

To avoid clogging your toilet, don't flush any paper *except* toilet paper down it. If it does clog up, however, try these methods in order.

Supplies
- bathroom plunger
- auger, or "snake" (can be rented)

What to Do

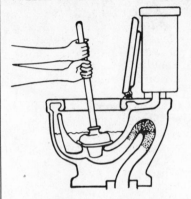

1. Use your rubber plunger, as described on the previous page, but don't pour boiling water into the toilet, since it might crack the bowl.

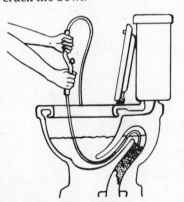

2. Work your auger into the drain hole of the toilet bowl, feeding it through until you

reach and push through the obstruction. Again, be careful not to crack the bowl with the metal auger.

Source: Plumbing-Heating-Cooling Information Bureau.

🔧 How to Fix a Running Toilet

If water continues to run into the toilet bowl after the toilet has been flushed and has refilled with water, check each of the following until you've fixed the problem.

Supplies

- screwdriver
- pliers
- wrench
- new parts (depending on what has to be replaced)

What do Do

1. Rubber tank ball. If the ball is worn out or misshapen, and if it fails to drop tightly into the hollowed discharge opening, it should be replaced with a new one or with a rubber flapper. To replace:

- Shut off water supply and empty the tank (or empty the tank and slide a stick under the float arm to shut off the supply valve and prevent the tank from refilling).

- Unscrew the ball from the lower lift wire and attach a new one of the same diameter. Or attach a flapper, which is available in hardware stores, to the base of the overflow tube and hook its chain to the trip lever.

2. Discharge opening. If the collar of the discharge opening is corroded or covered with grit, scrape and sand it until it's smooth.

3. Lift wires. Straighten or replace bent lift wires so that the tank ball drops squarely onto the hollowed discharge opening.

4. Float ball. If the float ball is leaky and waterlogged, it will not completely shut off the supply valve and water will continue to run into the tank. Replace it with a new one.

5. Float arm. If the float arm has become bent, it may either prevent the float from rising high enough to shut off the supply valve completely or it may let the float ball rise too high and allow water to drain into the overflow tube. Bend the arm until the problem is fixed and the supply valve completely shuts off.

Source: Plumbing-Heating-Cooling Information Bureau.

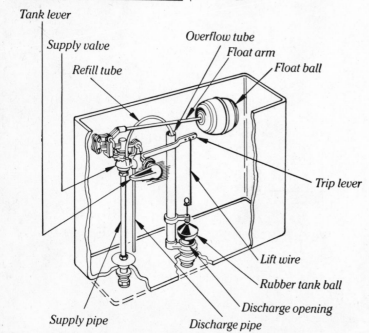

Tank lever
Supply valve
Refill tube
Overflow tube
Float arm
Float ball
Trip lever
Lift wire
Rubber tank ball
Discharge opening
Supply pipe
Discharge pipe

How to Replace a Broken Window

Supplies

- pliers
- putty knife
- putty or glazing compound
- new window glass
- glazier points
- hammer

What to Do

1. Work from the outside of the frame.

2. Remove the broken glass with pliers to avoid cutting your fingers.

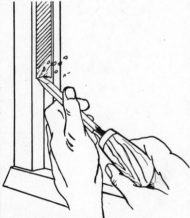

3. Remove old putty and glazier points.

4. Place a thin ribbon of putty in the frame.

5. Place glass firmly against the putty.

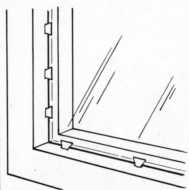

6. Insert glazier points. Tap in carefully to prevent breaking the glass. Points should be placed near the corners first, and then every 4–6″ along the glass.

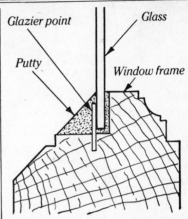

Glazier point   *Glass*
Putty   *Window frame*

7. Fill the groove with putty or glazing compound. Press it firmly against the glass with a putty knife or your fingers. Smooth the surface with the putty knife. The putty should form a smooth seal around the window.

Source: U.S. Dept. of Agriculture.

💡 How to Save Energy

11 Ways to Cut Your Heating Bill

1. Lower your thermostat to 65° during the day and 55° at night (clock thermostats can do that for you automatically). Add more clothing to compensate. A heavy sweater, for instance, gives you 4° more warmth.

2. Clean or replace your furnace filter once a month.

3. Make sure your home is adequately insulated.

4. Check your heating duct work once a year for leaks. Feel around the duct joints when the fan is on. Repair small leaks with duct tape. Caulk and tape larger ones.

5. Caulk windows (outside); weatherstrip windows and doors (inside).

6. Dust radiator surfaces often.

7. Close off attic and make sure the access door is weather-stripped.

8. Don't use your fireplace for supplemental heating when your furnace is on, unless you either:

• lower the thermostat to 50–55° to prevent costly heat loss through the fireplace vent; or,

• close all doors and warm air ducts entering the room with the fireplace and open a window near the fireplace about 1" to provide oxygen for the fire.

9. Make sure your water heater is adequately insulated.

10. Do as much household cleaning and washing as you can in warm or cold (not hot) water.

11. Turn your water heater to between 120–140°, unless you have a dishwasher, which requires 150° water.

6 Ways to Cut Your Cooling Bill

1. If you have an air conditioner, set your thermostat to 78°.

2. Clean or replace your air conditioner filter once a month.

3. Use a window fan with your window air conditioner to spread cooled air farther.

4. Keep lamps and TV sets away from your air conditioner's thermostat.

5. Do your cooking and use other heat-generating appliances in the early morning and late evening hours.

6. Keep windows, curtains and outside doors closed during the hottest hours of the day.

4 Ways to Cut Your Water Bill

1. Install an aerator in your kitchen and bathroom faucets—you'll use less water.

2. Fix leaky faucets and leaky and running toilets promptly.

3. Take showers rather than baths, but limit your showering time. It takes 30 gallons of water to fill the average tub; a 5-min. shower uses about 20 gallons.

4. Wash full loads of clothes in your washer and dishes in your dishwasher, but don't overload either machine.

8 Ways to Cut Your Light Bill

1. Reduce overall lighting in non-working areas by removing 1 bulb out of 3 in multiple light fixtures and replacing it with a burned-out bulb for safety.

2. Install solid-state dimmers or hi-low switches when replacing light switches.

3. Use 1 large bulb instead of several small ones where bright light is needed.

4. Place long-life incandescent lamps only in hard-to-reach places. They're less efficient than ordinary bulbs.

5. Use lamps with 3-way switches where you can, but only use the high switch for reading or other activities that require bright light. Always use the lowest level when you're watching television.

6. Use low-wattage night-light bulbs. They now come in 4-watt and 7-watt sizes.

7. Use fluorescent lights wherever you can; they give out more lumens per watt. (For example, a 40-watt fluorescent lamp gives off 80 lumens per watt and a 60-watt incandescent lamp gives off only 14.7.) Fluorescent lighting is effective for kitchen and bath areas.

8. Keep all lamps and fixtures clean.

11 Ways to Save Energy in the Kitchen

1. If you have a gas stove, make sure the pilot light is burning efficiently—with a blue flame. A yellowish flame needs adjustment.

2. Always bring water to a boil in a covered pan.

3. Match the size of the pan to the heating element—more heat will get to the pan.

4. If you cook with electricity, turn burners or oven off a few minutes before the allotted cooking time. The heating element will stay hot long enough to finish the job.

5. Cook as many foods in the oven as you can at one time.

6. Cook with a clock or timer; don't open the oven door continually to check food.

7. Use glass or ceramic pans for baking; you can reduce oven temperatures by 25°.

8. Use pressure cookers, microwaves or small electric pans or ovens when you can. They use less energy than your stove or oven.

9. Make sure refrigerator door seals are tight. Test them by closing the door over a dollar bill. If you can pull it out easily, the latch may need adjustment or the seal may need to be replaced.

10. Defrost the freezer when ice is ¼″ thick, and dust or vacuum the condenser coils at the back of the refrigerator a few times a year.

11. Let your dishes air dry after you've washed them in the dishwasher. If you don't have an automatic air-dry switch, turn off the control knob after the final rinse and prop the door open a little.

Source: U.S. Dept. of Energy.

⊙ Home Security Checklist

General Security

- [ ] Trim shrubs so that windows and doors are in full view from the street.
- [ ] Make sure you've got adequate outdoor lighting, especially at side and back doors.
- [ ] Don't leave "hidden" house keys nearby. Most hiding spots are well known to burglars.
- [ ] Make sure your mailbox is large enough to conceal your mail totally, or install a slot in the door.
- [ ] Display your house numbers prominently, and make sure they're well lighted.
- [ ] Make sure that all exterior doors are either metal-clad or solid hardwood.
- [ ] Install deadbolt locks on all exterior doors. Use a thumb turn (single-cylinder) lock when there's no breakable glass within 40″ of the lock; otherwise use a key (double-cylinder) lock.
- [ ] Secure sliding doors and supplement window locks.
- [ ] Install a wide-angle peephole in your front door; don't depend on an inside chain guard to protect you when you're identifying visitors.

Before You Go Away

- [ ] Ask a trusted neighbor to park in your driveway, put garbage in your garbage can, mow the lawn or shovel the sidewalk, and occasionally check your home.
- [ ] Have the post office hold your mail, and cancel the newspaper (rather than tell the paper company you're going on vacation).

Sources: National Bureau of Standards, Minnesota Dept. of Public Safety.

- [ ] Use automatic timers to turn lights on at dusk and off at your normal bedtime. Vary the lights to be turned on. Also have a timer turn a radio on occasionally during the day.
- [ ] Leave your drapes in the normal position and have a neighbor close them at night, open them at daylight and reposition them every day or so.
- [ ] Unplug your phone or set the bell on low to prevent a potential burglar from hearing an unanswered phone ring.
- [ ] Tell a neighbor where you can be reached in an emergency.
- [ ] For long absences, ask your local law enforcement agency to keep an eye on your home.

5 Ways to Secure a Sliding Door

1. Drill a downward-angled hole at the top center of the door's overlapping frames. Insert a steel pin or heavy nail in the hole.

2. Place a broomstick or a length of wood in the lower track. Make sure it's snug.

3. Buy a "Charley bar" from a locksmith. It attaches to the side frame and folds down across the glass, bracing itself against the opposite frame.

4. Install a special key-operated deadbolt lock.

5. Install 1¼" large-head, sheet metal screws in the upper track at both ends and in the middle. They should protrude just enough to let the sliding frame clear, but not enough to allow someone to pry the sliding door from its track.

3 Ways to Secure a Window

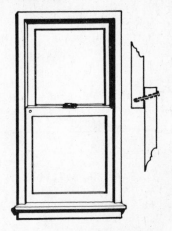

1. For traditional double-hung windows, drill a small hole at a slight downward angle through the first sash and into (but not through) the second sash. Then slip a heavy steel pin or large nail into the hole.

2. For windows that slide sideways, use the broomstick method described above.

3. For casement windows, remove the operator handle and store it in a convenient place. Even if someone breaks the glass, it will be difficult to reach inside and crank open the window.

Source: Minnesota Dept. of Public Safety.

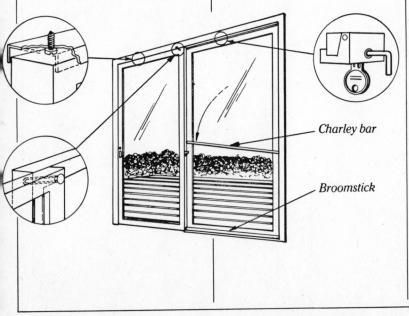

Charley bar

Broomstick

🏠 Spring and Fall Checklists

Spring

- [ ] Take off storms; hose and put up screens.
- [ ] Wash windows.
- [ ] Wash curtains and blankets.
- [ ] Wash walls, woodwork and ceilings.
- [ ] Have furnace serviced to take advantage of off-season rates; get chimney cleaned.

- [ ] Install room air conditioners; clean or replace filters.
- [ ] Clean out gutters and downspouts.
- [ ] Examine your roof for leaks.
- [ ] Check basement walls for cracks or leaks.
- [ ] Check siding and exterior paint.
- [ ] Rake and fertilize lawn; seed bare areas.

- [ ] Prune trees and shrubs; fertilize.
- [ ] Plant garden.
- [ ] Test and repair lawn mower.
- [ ] Clean out garage; clean patio and front porch.
- [ ] Clean outdoor furniture and barbecue grill.
- [ ] Mend, clean and store winter clothing; bring out summer clothes.

Fall

- [ ] Wash windows and put up storms.
- [ ] Caulk around windows where needed; check weatherstripping.
- [ ] Remove window air conditioners where possible; cover and insulate non-removable ones.

- [ ] Have furnace checked and serviced, if you didn't do this in the spring. Drain and refill radiator system, if necessary.
- [ ] Clean out gutters and downspouts.
- [ ] Turn off outside water faucets.
- [ ] Close off attic rooms.
- [ ] Rake lawn.

- [ ] Clean and store outdoor furniture, lawn care equipment.
- [ ] Clean, mend and store summer clothing; bring out winter clothes.
- [ ] Take an inventory of winter clothing you'll need and check for pre-season sales.

Chapter 6

CARING FOR YOUR HOUSEPLANTS

3 Ways to Water Your Plants

Here are 3 different watering methods you can use. Each has its advantages and disadvantages, so it's wise to alternate methods now and then. The first method, surface watering, is the most convenient and efficient. It's also the only way to water plants in pots that don't have drainage holes. Its disadvantage is that it can lead to overwatering. The next 2 methods—bottom watering and wick watering—are far less likely to result in overwatering. However, they can sometimes cause chemicals to gather on the soil's surface.

1. **Surface watering.** Pour water slowly over the surface until it starts to run out of the bottom of the container. Be careful not to wash away the soil from the crown and top roots of the plant.

2. **Bottom watering.** Pour water into a saucer underneath any pot with a bottom drainage hole. Capillary action of the plant's root system will move the water up through the potting mix until it reaches the surface. Remove excess water in the saucer in about an hour, when the soil's surface feels moist.

Occasionally pour water over the surface to dissolve chemicals that tend to gather on the surface.

3. **Wick watering.** When you pot the plant, insert an absorbent wick that reaches from the bottom drainage hole to the soil in the pot. Then follow the directions for bottom watering. The wick helps the plant's root system absorb moisture.

Tips on Watering Your Plants Properly

• **Before you water,** use a knitting needle to poke a few holes in the soil, allowing the water to penetrate the root ball adequately.

• **Drinking water** is usually safe to use in watering, since the chlorine level isn't high enough to hurt most plants. If your water is fluoridated, however, use untreated water.

• **Ferns and African violets** are sensitive to chlorine levels in drinking water, so these plants need water that's been exposed to air overnight, allowing the chlorine to escape into the atmosphere.

• **Water plants** in the morning with room-temperature water.

• **Growing or flowering plants** need more water than resting or dormant ones.

• **Plants with hairy, thorny or waxy leaves** need less water than thin-leaved varieties.

Sources: U.S. Dept. of Agriculture, U.S. Dept. of the Interior, New York State Cooperative Extension.

Potting Mixture

You can buy many kinds of prepackaged potting soils at garden stores and nurseries. You can also make your own using the recipes below. The charts on the following pages identify the soil requirements of various plants.

Regular: 1 part potting soil
1 part organic matter (rotted leaves, peat moss, sphagnum moss)
1 part coarse sand or perlite
1 tsp. 20% superphosphate per quart of mixture

Rich: Regular with extra part organic matter added.

Sandy: Regular, with extra part sand or perlite added.

Plant	Light/Sun	Water	Humidity	Temperature	Soil
African Violet *(Saintpaulia ionantha)*	Bright, indirect light for flowering; too much causes bleaching or burning. East or west windows are best.	Use "bottom watering" or "wick watering" methods; water only when soil *begins* to dry out.	Medium; don't mist.	65–75° F.	Rich.
Aloe	Full, direct sunlight.	Make sure soil is thoroughly dry before watering. Water 1–2 times a week in summer, once every 2–4 weeks in winter.	Low to medium.	50–60° F.	Regular.
Arrowhead Plant *(Symgonium podophyllum or Nephthytis)*	Medium to dim light.	Keep soil barely moist.	Medium to low.	Average household temperatures.	Regular.
Asparagus Fern *(Asparagus sprengeri)*	Bright, indirect sunlight. East or west windows are best.	Soak soil thoroughly with each watering; allow soil to dry thoroughly between waterings.	Medium; mist regularly.	60–68° F.	Regular.
Avocado *(Persea americana)*	Bright, indirect sun; leaves burn easily.	Keep soil moist; use tepid water when watering.	High to medium; mist regularly.	60–70° F.	Regular.
Baby Tears *(Helxine soleirolii)*	Indirect, filtered, low light from an east or north window.	Keep evenly moist.	High; mist often.	65–70° F.	Regular.
Boston Fern *(Nephrolepis exaltata)*	Bright, filtered light.	Keep evenly moist without letting roots get soggy or soil dry out.	High; mist daily.	60–70° F.	Rich.
Cactii	Full light.	Water once or twice a week in summer, once every 2–4 weeks in winter.	Low.	50–60° F. minimum.	Regular.

✿ Caring for Your Houseplants

Plant	Light/Sun	Water	Humidity	Temperature	Soil
Coleus	Leaves become most colorful when placed in plenty of sunshine.	Keep evenly moist.	Medium.	70–85° F.	Regular.
Croton *(Codiaeum)*	Will grow in shaded areas, but bright sunlight will bring out full color.	Keep evenly moist; never let soil dry out.	Medium.	60° F. minimum.	Regular.
Dieffenbachia, "Dumb Cane" *(Dieffenbachia maculata)*	2–3 hrs. of sunlight a day in an east or west window; other times, bright, indirect light.	Keep barely moist; let dry out for a few days before re-watering.	Medium; mist regularly.	Prefers warm temperatures.	Regular.
Dracaena	Indirect sun or bright light; no direct sunlight.	Keep evenly moist but not soggy. Water when soil feels dry to the touch.	Medium to high; mist daily.	60–70° F. Keep away from heating vents.	Sandy.
English Ivy *(Hedera helix)*	Bright light, but no direct sun.	Keep barely moist.	Medium; mist occasionally.	Cool.	Regular.
False Aralia *(Dizygotheca elegantissima)*	Semi-sunny to semi-shady. East or west windows are ideal.	Keep barely moist, damp but not soggy.	Medium.	Tolerates high temperatures if there is plenty of humidity.	Regular.
Grape Ivy *(Cissus rhombifolia)*	Medium to bright light or filtered sun.	Soak soil thoroughly when watering; then allow to dry out completely before re-watering.	Medium to high; mist frequently.	Tolerates a wide range of temperatures; increase humidity as temperature goes up.	Regular.

Caring for Your Houseplants 🌿

Plant	Light/Sun	Water	Humidity	Temperature	Soil
Jade Plant *(Crassula arborescens)*	Full sun with shade at midday.	Allow soil to remain dry for several days between waterings.	Low.	65–75° F., though will tolerate lower and higher temperatures.	Sandy.
Jerusalem Cherry *(Solanum pseudocapsicum)*	Either direct sun or bright light.	Keep moist and allow soil to dry only moderately between waterings.	Medium.	Cool.	Regular.
Norfolk Island Pine *(Araucaria excelsa)*	Filtered sunlight from an east or west window.	Provide efficient drainage and allow soil surface to dry before re-watering.	High; mist daily.	50–60° F.	Rich.
Parlor Palm *(Chamaedora elegans)*	Requires low exposure to indirect light.	Keep soil moist but not soggy between March and October; in winter, allow palm to dry out between waterings.	Mist regularly.	60–75° F.	Regular.
Peperomia	Indirect sunlight or bright, indirect light.	Allow to dry thoroughly between waterings; never allow it to stand in water.	Low.	Low, but not below 60° F.	Regular.
Philodendron, Heartleaf *(Philodendron cordatum)*	Any exposure produces growth; does best in well-lighted areas.	Keep moist and never allow to dry out; don't let water remain standing in pot.	Mist daily; wash leaves regularly.	Normal house and office temperatures.	Regular.
Philodendron, Split-leaf *(Philodendron pertusum "Monstera deliciosa")*	Bright, indirect lighting.	Soak thoroughly and allow soil surface to remain dry 1–2 days before re-watering.	Mist daily; wash leaves weekly.	65–75° F.	Regular.

✥ Caring for Your Houseplants

Plant	Light/Sun	Water	Humidity	Temperature	Soil
Poinsettia *(Euphorbia pulcherrima)*	Bright, direct sunlight.	Keep constantly moist, but don't allow it to get soggy.	Medium.	Between 60° and 75° F. Keep it cool at night and away from drafts.	Regular.
Pothos, "Devil's Ivy" *(Scindapsus aureus)*	Bright, indirect sunlight.	Allow soil to dry out moderately between waterings.	Low.	65–75° F.	Rich.
Prayer Plant *(Maranta leuconeura)*	Indirect sunlight or bright light.	Keep soil moist at all times.	Medium to high; mist occasionally.	65° F. minimum. Prefers warm temperatures.	Regular.
Purple Passion Plant, "Velvet Plant" *(Gynura aurantica)*	Direct or partial sunlight for full purple color.	Keep soil evenly moist.	Medium to high; mist frequently.	65–75° F.	Regular.
Rubber Plant *(Ficus elastica decora)*	Does best in well-lighted windows.	Water only when soil is completely dry; then water thoroughly.	Medium.	Any average household temperature.	Regular.
Schefflera, "Umbrella Tree" *(Schefflera venulosa)*	Does not like direct sunlight; does best in bright, filtered light.	Soak pot thoroughly; then let soil dry completely before re-watering.	High; mist daily with warm water.	55–75° F.	Regular.
Snake Plant *(Sansevieria trifasciata)*	Low light to grow; filtered sunlight to bloom.	Never overwater; plant likes dryness.	Low.	Normal household temperatures; don't allow sudden chills.	Regular.

Plant	Light/Sun	Water	Humidity	Temperature	Soil
Spider Plant *(Chlorophytum elatum vittatum)*	Indirect sun or moderately lighted areas.	Keep barely moist.	Medium to low.	Warm.	Regular.
Swedish Ivy *(Plectranthus australis)*	Diffused sun or bright light from a west or south window.	Keep moist but not soggy; allow to dry out slightly between waterings.	Medium; mist only if environment is very dry.	65° F. minimum.	Regular.
Wandering Jew *(Zebrina pendula)*	Bright, indirect sunlight.	Water generously, keeping soil moist at all times; during winter months, water less frequently.	Medium.	Warm.	Regular.
Weeping Fig *(Ficus benjamina)*	3 hrs. of direct light daily.	Water thoroughly once a week; never let soil dry out.	Medium; mist regularly.	Warm; 68–80° F.	Regular.
Zebra Plant *(Aphelandra squarrosa)*	Bright, indirect sun.	Water regularly; never let soil dry out.	High. Mist daily.	Warm and draft-free.	Rich.

Sources: U.S. Dept. of Agriculture, University of Minnesota Extension Service, New York State Cooperative Extension, U.S. Dept. of the Interior.

🌱 Plant Diagnostic Chart

Symptoms		Too much light	Not enough light	High temperature	Low temperature	Overwatering or poor drainage	Not enough water	Too much fertilizer	Not enough fertilizer	Compacted soil,	Drafts	Day length	Air pollution
Foliage:	tips or margins brown					●	●	●	●		●		
	bend down and curl				●						●		●
	yellowish green	●	●	●		●		●	●	●			●
	oldest drop		●	●		●	●	●	●	●	●		●
	all drop					●	●	●					●
	spots	●			●		●						
	wilt	●		●		●	●	●			●	●	
Growth:	weak, thin and soft		●	●					●	●			
	new leaves small		●	●		●	●	●	●	●			●
	none develops				●	●	●	●					
	plant died				●	●	●	●					
Flowers:	fail to develop or buds drop		●	●	●	●	●	●	●	●	●	●	●
	color less intense		●	●		●				●	●		
	decline too fast			●			●				●		●
	become smaller		●							●	●		
	no blooms		●	●								●	

Source: New York State Cooperative Extension.

Pest	What They Look Like	What They Do	How to Get Rid of Them
Aphids	• $\frac{1}{16}$–$\frac{1}{8}$" long. • Green, pink, red or black. • Rounded or pear-shaped bodies.	• Cluster on the undersides of leaves or on the stems of flowerbuds. • Suck out plant juices, stunting plant growth, producing curled and distorted leaves. • Excrete a sticky liquid, called honeydew, which attracts ants.	• Wash leaves with soapy water and a soft cloth. • Swab leaves with rubbing alcohol. • Handpick aphids from leaves. • Use commercial spray pesticides, following directions on product.
Mealy Bugs	• $\frac{3}{16}$" long. • Softbodied, with waxy covering; look like they're dusted with flour. • Some have tail-like waxy filaments.	• Cluster at stem and leaf joints. • Lay eggs in clusters enclosed in waxy or cottony material. • Suck out plant juices, stunting or killing the plant. • Excrete honeydew, which attracts ants.	• Wash leaves with soapy water and a soft cloth. • Swab leaves with rubbing alcohol. • Handpick mealy bugs from leaves. • Isolate treated plants to avoid reinfestation.
Scales	• $\frac{1}{16}$–$\frac{1}{8}$" long. • Oval in shape. • Have a shell-like covering or scale that protects the entire body. • Colors range from black to white.	• Infest leaves or stems. • Lay eggs in a whitish sac. • Suck plant juices, stunting or killing the plant. • Excrete honeydew, which attracts ants.	• Discard heavily infested plants. • Wash with soapy water if infestation is limited to 1 or 2 plants.
Spider Mites	• Very small, oval in shape—barely visible to the naked eye. • Green, yellow or red.	• Infest undersides of leaves, then spread to other parts. • Feed on plant juices, causing white or yellow speckles to appear on leaves; leaves eventually turn bronze or yellow and drop off. • Form a frail, silky webbing that stretches from leaf to leaf.	• Syringe plants with a forceful spray of water to break up webbing and dislodge mites. • Spray with commercial pesticide following directions on product.
White Flies	• **Adults**—$\frac{1}{16}$" long; have white, wedge-shaped wings. • **Young**—oval, green, yellow or whitish.	• Feed on leaves of plant; suck juices, causing leaves to become pale, turn yellow and drop off. • Excrete sticky liquid. • Hatch eggs on undersides of leaves.	• Spray plants, especially undersides of leaves, with commercial pesticide, following directions on product.

Source: U.S. Dept. of Agriculture.

KEEPING RECORDS

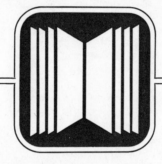

You may not want to write on the forms you'll find in this chapter. So either photocopy the ones you want or construct your own forms, using these as models. In both cases you'll be preserving the original for later use.

How to Keep Financial Records

Keep your home records in one of two places: in an *active file* (a drawer or storage box that will hold manila folders) or in *dead storage* (a chest or box in your attic or storeroom).

Active file

Your active files will probably contain items like the following, although you may wish to categorize them somewhat differently.

- **Cancelled checks and bank statements** for the past 3 years
- **Miscellaneous proofs of purchase,** such as paid bill receipts
- **Past net worth statements** (see pp. 150–151).
- **Medical records**
  - children's immunization records (see p.165)
  - receipts and cancelled checks for medical and dental bills
  - prescription numbers
- **Home management materials**
  - warranties, service contracts and operating instructions
  - current inventory of household items (see pp. 158–159)

- **Housing records**
  - copy of your mortgage, if possible
  - cancelled checks showing purchase costs and/or selling costs
  - information related to home improvements, such as cancelled checks, receipts, contracts
- **Insurance information**
  - copies or originals of all policies (life, medical, automobile, homeowner's and personal property)
  - names, phone numbers and addresses of agents
- **Credit information,** including copies of all loan agreements, promissory notes, statements and receipts from each account
- **Investment transaction records,** including stock certificates and broker's confirmations of purchases and sales
- **Wills and estate planning records**
  - an unsigned copy of the original will and a note giving the location of the original
  - instructions regarding final services and the location of the burial plot
  - names and addresses of lawyer and executor
- **Education records**

- **Safe-deposit box folder,** with a list of all the items stored in it and the location of the key (see next page)
- **Tax records**
  - state, federal and personal property tax forms (for at least 3 years)
  - records of deductible business and professional expenses
  - records of the interest paid on mortgage loans and others
  - records of medical bills (once deducted)
  - records of capital gains and losses
  - records of casualty losses
  - records of contributions
  - bills of sale for large-ticket items, like a car

After 3 years, this information should be refiled in dead storage for at least 3 more years (because you can be audited back to 6 years ago). After this time your records cannot be subpoenaed unless fraud is involved.

Dead storage file

In your dead storage file, keep those old records that you may never need but should have on hand just in case.

- **Superseded legal papers**
- **Tax information and cancelled checks** that date back at least 7 years

Safe-Deposit Box

This is the place to keep irreplaceable or difficult-to-replace items, as well as small valuables. A couple might consider renting 2 of them—in the event of death or legal difficulties, the contents of one box could be tied up for some time by the courts. You should store the following in your box:

☐ **Leases**

☐ **List of insurance policies,** their numbers and companies

☐ **Stocks and bond certificates,** certificates of deposit or other bank savings certificates

☐ **Automobile title** and any other titles

☐ **Property records,** titles and deeds, including mortgage

☐ **Important receipts** and major bills of sale

☐ **Legal papers, contracts**

☐ **Copy of household inventory,** including photos (see pp. 158–159)

☐ **Personal papers**
- birth, marriage and death certificates
- divorce decrees
- adoption papers
- citizenship papers
- military service records

Source: This information taken from the booklet, "Your Financial Plan," published by the Money Management Inst. of Household Finance Corp., Prospect Heights, Illinois.

Important Numbers to Record
Major Credit Cards

Number

_____   _____
_____   _____
_____   _____
_____   _____

Bank Accounts

_____   _____
_____   _____
_____   _____

Insurance Policies

_____   _____
_____   _____
_____   _____

📖 Net Worth Statement

How to Figure Out
Your Net Worth

Date _____

What you own

Cash in checking accounts	$ _____
Cash in savings accounts	_____
Current value of government savings bonds	_____
Cash surrender value of insurance policies	_____
Equity in pensions	_____
Equity in profit-sharing plans	_____
Current value of annuities	_____
Loans owed you	_____

Retirement funds

Individual Retirement Account or	
Keogh Plan (U.S.)	_____
Registered Retirement Savings Plan (Canada)	_____
Tax refunds due	_____
Cash value of ownership in a business	_____

Market value of securities

Bonds	_____
Stocks	_____
Mutual funds	_____
Investment trusts	_____

Cash value of personal property

Home and other real estate	_____
Car(s)	_____
Furniture	_____
Appliances	_____
Other (furs, jewelry, antiques, fine art, etc.)	_____

Other assets

_____   _____

_____   _____

Total Assets .... $ _____

Net Worth Statement 📖

What you owe

Mortgage debts (home and other real estate) . . . . _____

Installment debts (balance due on car,
   furniture, appliances, etc.) . . . . _____

Personal loans . . . . _____

Current bills outstanding . . . . _____

Taxes due . . . . _____

Other liabilities

Total Liabilities . . . . $ _____

Your Net Worth (assets minus liabilities) . . . . $ _____

Source: This chart taken from the booklet, "Your Financial Plan," published by the Money Management Inst. of Household Finance Corp., Prospect Heights, Illinois.

📖 How to Prepare a Household Budget

Preparing a budget involves estimating your income and expenses for certain periods of time. When you do this, you should take 3 different kinds of expenses into account:

Fixed expenses. Fixed expenses are those you have promised to pay on *specific* dates and in *specific* amounts. Some of these—rent and mortgage payments, installment debts—are paid each month. Others are paid only once, twice or seasonally during the year—for example, insurance premiums, taxes, school tuition and auto license plates. (See the next page for a list of typical fixed expenses.)

• Periodic expenses. Periodic expenses are really fixed expenses that are so large that payments cannot be made from a single paycheck (for taxes, tuition and so on). Therefore, a certain amount of money must be set aside during each planning period to meet them.

• Flexible expenses. Flexible expenses vary both in amount and in the planning period in which they are needed. Some occur each planning period, like food and transportation, for example. Other expenses—clothing, entertainment, medical—may occur less often or change seasonally. (See the next page for a list of typical flexible expenses.)

Steps to take

1. **Estimate your income and your fixed, periodic and flexible expenses** for 2 or 3 planning periods (usually months) at a time.
- Use old receipts, cancelled checks, paid bills and other documents to remind you of what you've spent in the past.
- Determine what your large periodic expenses for the year are and how much you'll need to set aside each planning period.
- Record these figures on the planning forms on pp. 154–157.

2. **Record your actual income and expenses** for these periods.

3. **Revise your budget for the next 2 or 3 planning periods.**

4. **As you gain experience, you'll be able to extend your budget** to cover an additional 1–6 months longer.

How to Prepare a Household Budget 📖

Fixed Expenses

Housing
- Rent
- Mortgage payments
- Maintenance fee

Taxes
- Federal income tax*
- State income tax*
- Local taxes
- Property taxes

Utilities and Home Services
- Telephone
- Gas
- Water
- Fuel

- Sewage
- Garbage pickup
- Cable TV

Installment Payments
- Automobile
- Furniture or appliances
- Personal loans

Insurance
- Life
- Automobile
- Health and accident
- Hospitalization
- Fire and theft
- Personal property

*Estimate any additional payment
beyond amount withheld from wages.

- Social security

Fees for Education
- Tuition, books
- Room and Board

Transportation
- Automobile license plates
- Vehicle sticker
- Commuting fare
- Parking
- Garage rental

Personal Allowances
- Husband
- Wife
- Children

Membership Dues
- Union
- Professional associations
- Clubs

Contributions
- Religious
- Charity

Savings
- Emergency fund
- For goals

Subscriptions

Flexible Expenses

Food
- Meals at home
- Meals eaten out

Clothing
- New clothes
- Laundry, drycleaning
- Repairs and alterations

Household Equipment
- Appliances
- Furniture
- Repairs

Home Improvement
- Maintenance
- Remodeling

Household Supplies
- Cleaning supplies
- Small items for the home
- First-aid supplies

Household Help
- Baby sitter
- Yard care
- Housecleaning

Gift
- Birthdays
- Weddings, anniversaries
- Religious celebrations
- Showers
- Illness
- Graduation

Transportation
- Gasoline
- Repairs and upkeep
- Taxi
- Bus or train

Contributions
- Religious

- Charities
- Service groups
- Professional groups
- Fraternal groups
- Social clubs
- Schools and colleges

Health
(not covered by insurance)
- Medical
- Dental
- Eye care/glasses
- Prescription drugs

Personal Care
- Grooming aids
- Barber shop
- Beauty parlor

Entertainment
- Parties

- Theater tickets
- Sports events

Recreation
- Hobbies
- Vacation
- Sports equipment

Miscellaneous
- Papers, magazines
- Books
- Stationery, postage
- Tobacco

Source: This information taken from the booklet, "Your Financial Plan," published by the Money Management Inst. of Household Finance Corp., Prospect Heights, Illinois.

◫ How to Prepare a Household Budget

Income

Planning Periods	Jan.	Feb.	March	April	May
Sources of Income					
Total Income					

Fixed Expenses

Planning Periods	Jan.		Feb.		March		April		May	
Fixed Expenses	Planned	Actual	Planned	Actual	Planned	Actual	Planned	Actual	Planned	Actual
Total Fixed Expenses										

June	July	August	Sept.	Oct.	Nov.	Dec.

June		July		August		Sept.		Oct.		Nov.		Dec.	
Planned	Actual	Planned	Actual	Planned	Actual	Planned	Actual	Planned	Actual	Planned	Actual	Planned	Actual

📖 How to Prepare a Household Budget

Flexible Expenses

Planning Periods	Jan.		Feb.		March		April		May	
Flexible Expenses	Planned	Actual	Planned	Actual	Planned	Actual	Planned	Actual	Planned	Actual
Total Flexible Expenses										

Periodic Expenses

Planning Periods		Jan.		Feb.		March		April		May	
Periodic Expenses	**Yearly Total**	Planned	Actual	Planned	Actual	Planned	Actual	Planned	Actual	Planned	Actual
Total Periodic Expenses											

Yearly Total ÷ Number of Planning Periods = Amount to set Aside Each Planning Period

_____ ÷ _____ = _____

June		July		August		Sept.		Oct.		Nov.		Dec.	
Planned	Actual	Planned	Actual	Planned	Actual	Planned	Actual	Planned	Actual	Planned	Actual	Planned	Actual

June		July		August		Sept.		Oct.		Nov.		Dec.	
Planned	Actual	Planned	Actual	Planned	Actual	Planned	Actual	Planned	Actual	Planned	Actual	Planned	Actual

📖 How to Take a Household Inventory

An up-to-date inventory of your household furnishings and personal belongings can help you to:

- Determine the value of your belongings and your personal insurance needs.

- Establish the purchase dates and cost of major items in the case of a loss and identify exactly what was lost.

- Verify losses for income tax deductions.

Steps to take

1. **List major items** in each room of the house. Note serial numbers, purchase prices, present value and dates of purchase where possible. Attach any available receipts.

2. **To back up the inventory, photograph each wall of each room** with closet or cabinet doors open. On the back of each picture, write the date, the general location and the contents shown.

3. **Store the inventory and photographs** in your safe deposit box.

4. **Keep a copy** of the inventory and the negatives of the photographs at home so that you can update the inventory from time to time.

Inventory Form

Article/Room	Description/Serial No.	Purchase Date	Purchase Price

How to Take a Household Inventory 📖

Article/Room	Description/Serial No.	Purchase Date	Purchase Price

Source: Insurance Information Institute.

📖 How to Keep Family Health Records

Family health records have a number of valuable uses.

• They record important data that children will need later in their lives.

• They make it easier to consult new doctors.

• They help you avoid the expense of duplicating previous tests and procedures.

• They could save your life by averting the use of anesthetics or prescription medicines that you are allergic to or that could react violently with medications you'ure already taking.

Use the following forms to keep your family's records up-to-date and accessible.

Family History

Family Members (blood relations)	Lifestyle		
	Type of Work	Work-Related Hazards/Pathogens (DDT, mercury, etc.)	Stressful Events or Conditions (business problems, family problems, military duties, alcohol/chemical dependencies, etc.)
Grandparents			

Family Members (blood relations)	Lifestyle (continued)		
	Type of Work	**Work-Related Hazards/Pathogens** (DDT, mercury, etc.)	**Stressful Events or Conditions** (business problems, family problems, military duties, alcohol/chemical dependencies, etc.)
Parents			
Siblings			
Children			

📖 How to Keep Family Health Records

Family Members (blood relations)	Disease History										
	Allergies	Diabetes	Drug Abuse (incl. alcoholism)	Emotional Problem(s)	Heart Problem(s)	Hypertension	Stroke	Ulcers	Other	If Deceased, Age at Death	Cause of Death
Grandparents											
Parents											

Family Members (blood relations)	Disease History (continued)										
	Allergies	Diabetes	Drug Abuse (incl. alcoholism)	Emotional Problem(s)	Heart Problem(s)	Hypertension	Stroke	Ulcers	Other	If Deceased, Age at Death	Cause of Death
Siblings											
Children											

Birth Records

Name	Date of Birth	Weight at Birth	Length at Birth	Mother's Health in Pregnancy (illnesses, drugs, problems)	Delivery (normal/ abnormal)	Condition at Birth	Feeding Method (breast /bottle)	Blood Type/Rh
Mother								
Father								
Children 1.								
2.								
3.								
4.								
5.								

Immunizations and Disease Chart

Names			Father	Mother	Children		
			Date or Imm.	Date or Imm.	Date or Imm.	Date or Imm.	Date or Imm.
DPT	Diptheria	First					
		Second					
		Third					
	Tetanus	Boosters					
	Whooping Cough						
Polio		First					
		Second					
		Third					
		Boosters					
Rubella							
Measles							
Mumps							
Chickenpox							
Hepatitis							
Strep Throat							
Scarlet Fever							
Rheumatic Fever							
Tuberculosis (note tests for)							
Other							

Medications History

Family Member	Date	Problem	Medication Used (inc. strength of dosage)	Result/ Comment	Allergic Reaction?

Important Medical Events Record

Family Member	Date	Age	What Happened (including complications)	Physician

Lab Report Record

Family Member

Date

Blood Count (CBC)
    Hemoglobin

    Hematocrit

    WBC

    Differential

    RBC

    Sed. rate

Family Member

Date

Blood Chemistry
    Glucose

    Triglycerides

    Cholesterol

    Uric acid

    Other (list)

Family Member

Date

Urinalysis

Family Member

Date

**Electrocardiogram
(EKG)**

Family Member _____
        Date _____

X-Ray (type) _____

Family Member _____
        Date _____

Pap Test _____

Family Member _____
        Date _____

Other _____

Directory of Family Members' Doctors

Use this directory to record information about all the doctors your family goes to. Keep changes up-to-date so medical records can be located and referred to quickly.

Family Member	Doctor's Name, Address and Phone Number	Type of Doctor	Date Started with Doctor	Date Ended with Doctor
1. _____				
2. _____				
3. _____				
4. _____				
5. _____				

Source: *The Family Doctor's Health Tips,* Keith Sehnert, M.D. (Meadowbrook Press, 1981).

Index

Floors, cleaning, 22
Food labels, 81
Fractures, 99
Frostbite, 104
Fruit
  buying, 34–40
  caloric countent of, 92–93
  nutritional value of, 72, 74–76, 78–80, 83, 86
  servings, 50
  storing, 34–40, 45
Furniture, cleaning, 20–21
Fuses, replacing, 124–125

G

Grains
  caloric content of, 95
  nutritional value of, 72, 76–77, 79–80

H

Health records, 160–170
  see also Records
Heart attacks, 104
Heat exhaustion, 105
Heat stroke, 105
Herbs and spices, uses of, 63–67
Home security, 134–135
Household records, 148
  see also Records
Houseplants, 138–145
  care of, 139–143
  controlling pests, 145
  diagnosing problems, 144–145
  potting mixtures, 138
  watering, 138
Hurricanes, 116
Hypothermia, 105

I

Inventory, household, 158–159
  see also Records

L

Lampshades, cleaning, 19
Leather, cleaning, 20

M

Maintenance, home, 120–136
Measurements, cooking, 51
Medical records
  see Health records
Meat
  caloric content of, 89–90
  cooking, 52–54, 56–57
  nutritional value of, 73–75, 77, 79–80, 83, 86
  servings, 50
  storing, 44
  see also Poultry
Minerals, 79–80, 82–83

N

Net worth statement, 148, 150–151
Nutrients, basic, 74–80, 82–83
Nutrition, 72–96
Nuts
  caloric content of, 90
  cooking, 43
  nutritional value of, 72, 74, 79–80, 83
  storing, 43

O

Ovens, cleaning, 16

P

Pasta (noodles)
  caloric content of, 95
  cooking, 40
Phone numbers, emergency
  home repair, 120
  medical, 98
Plants
  see Houseplants
Plastic counter tops, cleaning, 17
Poison ivy, oak, sumac, 107
Poisoning, 106–107
Poultry
  caloric content of, 90
  cooking, 55
  nutritional value of, 73, 77, 79, 83
  servings, 50
  storing, 44
Protein, 74–75, 83

R

Records
  financial, 148–157
  health, 160–170
  inventory, 158–159
Refrigerators, cleaning, 16–17
Repairs, home, 120–136
Rice
  caloric content of, 95
  cooking, 42
  nutritional value of, 72, 74, 78

S

Safe-deposit box, 148–149
Safety, 108
  see also Emergencies, First aid
Salt
  see Sodium
Saving energy, 132–133

Free Stuff!

FREE STUFF FOR TRAVELERS

Over 1,000 of the best free and up-to-a-dollar publications and products travelers can get by mail:
- guidebooks to cities, states & foreign countries
- pamphlets on attractions, festivals & parks
- posters, calendars & maps

$3.75 ppd.

FREE STUFF FOR COOKS

Over 250 of the best free and up-to-a-dollar booklets and samples cooks can get by mail:
- cookbooks & recipe cards
- money-saving shopping guides
- seeds & spices

$3.75 ppd.

FREE STUFF FOR KIDS

Over 250 of the best free and up-to-a-dollar things kids can get by mail:
- coins & stamps
- bumper stickers & decals
- posters & maps

$3.75 ppd.

FREE STUFF FOR HOME & GARDEN

Over 350 of the best free and up-to-a-dollar booklets and samples homeowners and gardeners can get by mail:
- booklets on home improvement & saving energy
- plans for do-it-yourself projects
- sample seeds

$3.75 ppd.

THE BEST FREE ATTRACTIONS SOUTH

From North Carolina to Texas, it's a land swarming with surprises – and over 1,500 of them free:
- alligator and turtle stalking
- cow chip tosses & mule races
- free watermelon, bluegrass & barbeque!

$4.75 ppd.

THE BEST FREE ATTRACTIONS WEST

Just passing through from California to Montana? It's all free and there for the asking:
- belching volcanoes & miniature forests
- gold panning & quarter horse racing
- vineyard tours and free wine samples!

$4.75 ppd.

THE BEST FREE ATTRACTIONS MIDWEST

From Kentucky to North Dakota, The Midwest is chock-full of free things:
- camel rides and shark feedings
- stagecoaches and magic tricks
- hobo conventions – and free Mulligan stew!

$4.75 ppd.

THE BEST FREE ATTRACTIONS EAST

Over 1,500 irresistible attractions – all free – from West Virginia to Maine (the proper East Coast):
- a witch-trial courthouse with evidence
- aviaries where **you** are caged
- the "gentle giants" – and free beer!

$4.75 ppd.